Summat & Nowt

Memories of a Yorkshire Editor

W R (Bill) Mitchell is in celebratory mood, having completed 50 years' association with The Dalesman, the oldest and most popular of the Yorkshire magazines and one which is read by exiles in every country on earth. He retired as Editor in 1988 but writes a monthly article, has the honorary title of Editorial Advisor. Bill's long service to north-country journalism and the community was acknowledged by the award of the MBE in the Queen's birthday honours and by an honorary degree of Doctor of Letters from the University of Bradford. He also holds honorary membership of the Yorkshire Dales Society.

Summat & Nowt

Memories of a Yorkshire Editor

by W R Mitchell

Illustrated by Richard Bancroft

CASTLEBERG
1998

"Don't worry about owt that'll mend." (A dalesman's words to a man fretting about his roof slates).

"Were there any old characters in Hawes?" I asked Jack Moore. He replied: "There were nowt else at one time."

"I was called after mi grandmother," said Horner Lambert of Aysgarth. "I used to tell mother a thing or two for giving me such a daft name, but she said it was either to be Horner or Moses, so I couldn't complain."

The Dales I first knew were teeming with rich characters. The higher up the dale you went, the more unique, and nicer, was the type of person you met. (James Herriot, talking to the author, 1990).

A **Castleberg** Book.

First published in the United Kingdom in 1998.

Text, © W R Mitchell 1998.

The moral right of the author has been asserted.

ISBN 1 871064 68 6

Typeset in Palatino, printed and bound in the United Kingdom by Lamberts Print & Design, Station Road, Settle, North Yorkshire, BD24 9AA.

Published by Castleberg, 18 Yealand Avenue, Giggleswick, Settle, North Yorkshire, BD24 0AY.

Contents

Additional illustrations – Steve Burke, 23; Godfrey Wilson, 26, 77; Peter Fox, 137.

The Road to Gordale Scar, Malhamdale.

Foreword

by

Richard Whiteley

Presenter of TV's "Countdown"

Four poignant words are used by Bill Mitchell in his introduction to this definitive work. "My Dales are dead."

I have news for you, Bill. Not while you or your written words are around, they're not.

Yes, things have changed. And you don't have to be a Dalesman of Bill's vintage and venerability to notice that. A new phone box here, a satellite dish there, a new car park, visitor centre, take away, video shop, radio mast, barn conversion – change is seen every year.

And yet, and yet. Go to an auction on market day. Linger outside a chapel on a Sunday. Call in on a remote pub late at night, peruse the village paragraphs in those charming country newspapers, such devoted chronicles of Dales life – do all this and you'll see that much of what Bill savours is very much alive.

Of course, those old days and old ways are disappearing but we are fortunate indeed that they have been recorded as meticulously and personally by Bill Mitchell.

In this volume are to be found characters a-plenty, copious humour, fascinating facts, but, above all, there is love.

To share that love of the dales is Bill Mitchell's great talent. He shares it generously and happily.

I hope that the work, with its autobiographical element, is not regarded by Bill as his grand finale. Let us hope that "Summat and Nowt" is not his summit and that there is more to come.

A Breezy Day in February.

In the Beginning

My Yorkshire Dales is dead. Or should it be *are* dead? Life in the dale-country as I first knew it has been transformed. Gone are the peaceful days, the cycling farmers and the walking postmen; gone the paraffin lamps and the hay rakes; gone the Shorthorn cow, hand-milking, corncrakes on night-shift and donkeys which transported the milk at Redmire. Most of my original Dales friends have "gone to their reward", as t'owd Methodists used to say. In this book, they are remembered with affection.

When the oldest amang 'em were alive and kicking, the Dales were so quiet they could hear the wax crackling in their ears. The daily round was hard, unremitting, and singularly free of stress of the nerve-twitching variety. I knew an old farmer who began every day by drinking a basin full of warm fat. He worked himself to death and didn't die of clogged-up arteries.

The Sabbath hush was such you could hear the murmuration of insects above the beating of your heart. The infernal-combustion engine was not shattering the peace. In a pre-electric age, when a cloud drifted across the moon, an old chap at Feizor declared: "T'village lantern's gone out." Forty years ago, Rupert Hart-Davis, standing in front of his primitive holiday cottage on the flanks of Kisdon Hill, in Swaledale, saw just one electric light – and that was in the telephone kiosk at Keld.

In the upper dales there were hardly any off-comers, apart from t'parsons, who changed over infrequently. The town of Settle, isolated from other towns by miles of dusty road, was unusual in having a genetic mix – the old Dales stock infused with the blood of imported labour, from all parts of the land, brought in to work in quarry and mill. Others arrived to help build the Settle-Carlisle railway and, after the war, the immigrants included dark-haired Spanish lasses, as domestics for Giggleswick School, soon to marry local men and learn how to make plain Yorkshire fare.

The daleheaders, in pre-wireless days, kept up-to-date with local gossip by going to market once a week or ordering a daily newspaper by post, ensuring regular visits on foot or bike by the local postman. Mrs Brown, of Cosh Farm, from which no other human residence might be seen, invited any ramblers to have cups of tea, her object being to learn more about the outer world.

The rambler was uncommon and, just after the 1939-45 war, was distinctive in his ex-Army clothing, including waterproof cape and studded boots. The 1920s and early 30s were the heyday of cycling when no place – not even Tan Hill Inn, a solitary building beside an upland road – was inaccessible. Lancashire cyclists might call at Malham on their homeward way, here to purchase pieces of rich fruit cake, to sustain them on the last few miles. Otherwise they would suffer from "hunger-knock" leading, if unattended, to a state of exhaustion known as "bonk".

I originally toured the Dales using one of the many buses or travelling on trains. The nearest railway station, at Clapham, was one and a-half miles from the village, but gave access to the Lancaster-Carlisle line, via a branch line through Ingleton, or to the Settle-Carlisle, if you walked from Giggleswick to Settle or booked through to Long Preston. I purchased a Bantam motor bike, lifted it into the guard's van, and extended my scope as a day-tripper.

Jim Taylor, stationmaster at Settle, was understanding. He also told about events on the afternoon of market day, which is Tuesday. He would emerge from his office to see the platforms littered with bulky objects, even the odd roll of linoleum. Whoever owned them had not gone through the formality of paying the carriage, but the people on the platform seemed to disown the goods – until the train appeared, when there would be a rush to gather them up and carry them into the compartments. At this stage, it was too late to do anything about it.

My first car was a Ford, 1939 vintage. The men at the Clapham garage stared at it with amazement when I arrived for a service, and proclaimed it had tappet-rattle, piston-slap, a crack on the port side of the chassis – and corroded engine mounts. When the flooring became badly worn and had to be replaced, a friend did the work, unwisely using a composition board, which reacted badly to the wet weather. On a trip up t'Dales, during the monsoon period, I had a sinking feeling and looked down through a gap in the board to see the roadway. A garageman in the nearest town fitted wooden floorboards while I waited. He creosoted them, at no extra charge.

The Dales had their lively moments, such as the show-day at Clapham when, as a young journalist, I secured all the winners of the horse-races before the first race had taken place. It was the year the bookies were "cleaned out" and departed leaving a stack of IOUs. There were riotous moments at village "hops", when dozens of clod-hopping farm men and their girls trampled the sedate aspects from old-tyme dancing, to music provided by piano accordion and drums. A dance did not warm-up until many of the men had sunk a few pints at the local inn.

At Tosside, I met Harry Cockerill, accordionist. He was self-taught, perfecting his technique at High Greenfield, a solitary farm on what had been the packhorse road from Wharfedale to Ribblesdale. When his father moved to a farm in Bishopdale, and before Harry had married, "I lived by missen for six years. Being one and a-half miles from t'next door neighbour, I found it was ideal for practicing the accordion." Harry went to his first dances on a motor bike, with the accordion in its case. It was attached to the bike using bands made to tie-up cows in the shippon.

Half a century ago, mechanisation had not yet transformed farm life in the Dales. Fordsons appeared during the 1939-45 war and drew ploughs which ripped up ancient grazing land. Then we had "lile grey Fergies", handy little tractors, regarded with awe by some and with love where they were used to take a hill farmer to and from the pub in an evening. Nearly every farm had a resident farm man, sometimes two men. Large families were the rule. An old friend used to say: "We'd not much else to do at night afore we got t'wireless."

Church and chapel, like cheese and chalk in the pre-ecumenical days, had no shortage of support. Village schools were numerous. Some farm children walked several miles a day, to and from school, and ate a few sandwiches at mid-day. The village shop sold virtually everything. One customer asked: "Do you sell fire-lighters?" The shop-keeper nodded. "Do you sell paraffin?" Another nod. "Then wash your hands and give me a few slices of boiled ham."

When I began to help Handby Ewbank with haytime, he worked in conjunction with Frank Lambert, who remembered when conditions for farm men were so bad that at some farms they only entered the house at meal-times and to sleep. In winter, the best way to keep warm was to go into a shippon and put your hands on the backs of the cows. Frank had a horse called Peggy which drew some primitive machines.

Most operations were labour-intensive. Joining a group engaged in hand-turning swathes, I was ribbed for not "odding t'rake reight" and was chided because hands unfamilar with hard physical toil had blisters growing on blisters. I was leading too soft a life.

I wrote a piece for *Dalesman* about George, t'battery man. He ensured that those living at remote farms and villages were able to listen to sensible things on the wireless, such as *Saturday Night Theatre*. The whole family, having changed into their better clothes, would silently listen. Those in the northern dales still spoke about t'time in the 1930s when t'Swaledale Singers went by taxi to Leeds and sang on t'wireless.

Women's Institutes thrived. Young Farmers' Clubs gave taciturn farm lads the "gift of the gab" and were also matrimonial agencies, introducing a lad from one dale to a lass in the next dale. Local government cost next to nowt and was truly local. At Hawes, there were two officials in an upstairs office, plus a girl to type the letters and make the tea.

My Yorkshire Dales are seen, in retrospect, as a time of innocence. Television had not brought big-city morality into the remotest rural corners. The only pornographic item that appeared in *The Dalesman* concerned a farmer who asked a friend: "What do you think about all this pornography?" The friend replied: "Nay – I don't know. I haven't got a pornograph." Satire had not robbed us of our respect for authority and religion, though *The Dalesman* carried quite a few acceptable chapel stories, such as that of the Sunday School teacher who, after telling her class about Jacob's vision of a ladder on which angels ascended and descended, was asked by a small boy why the angels needed a ladder when "they've getten wings". A girl from a dalehead farm suggested: "Appen they were in t'moult, miss."

The Media had yet to arise and create a modern Tower of Babel. In 1948, there was talk of a Yorkshire Dales National Park, whatever that was. Who'd heard of parks in t'countryside? Those who were anxious to preserve the greenest and most pleasant aspects of Old England were supporting the National Trust. In Lakeland, where they had been active for many years, Cubby Acland and a secretary were concerned with the day-to-day running of regional properties. In the Dales, there was nobbut one property, Stainforth Bridge, which had been handed over to the Trust by the Maudsleys of Knight Stainforth Hall and spanned the Ribble in a single graceful arch.

The Dalesman was for a time the only monthly magazine in the county. Now there's a torrent of material – books, maps, guides, videos. Newspaper features extol the beauties of the Dales. Television holiday programmes "do" the Dales in 10 minutes. The once derisory term "off-comer" is rarely heard now that "new settlers" are gaining the numerical ascendancy. They have played a significant part in modern cultural and social life.

Day-trippers are ubiquitous, some attached to a car park by umbilical cord, venturing in search of toilets and tea. Mostly, the visitors enjoy the Dales energetically, as walkers. At Kettlewell, and elsewhere, the summer sun brings a responsive gleam from acres of parked cars. I

Skipton on Market Day

14

mention Kettlewell because in the 1930s, J B Priestley told of a woman living at a farm who had visited this Wharfedale village each week for years but suddenly stopped doing so. As she explained to a friend: "I can't stand t'racket".

A native of Bradford, Jolly Jack Priestley requested that his ashes should be buried in the churchyard at Hubberholme. And so they were. I attended the interment, on a day when – to quote a local farmer – "t'day looks as if it's bin up all neet". It was lambing time, cold and clashy, and so most of the farmers had remained at home, ready to give succour to ailing lambs. Priestley's ashes, in their small container, had been in the area for a week or more, having been handed over to the safe keeping of a farmer until the funeral day. He had placed them in what he considered to be a dry and safe place – under the stairs. If there is a state of immortality, then Priestley must have chuckled over that.

At a time when anthropologists were trudging into wild and distant places, studying the natives, I set myself the task of recording Dales life from the lips of those who had experienced it. I had the advantage of having been born at Skipton, which proclaims itself as "gateway" to the Dales. Most commentators about Dales life have been off-comers. Folk tales were of special interest to me for they do not survive as do written records. Every old chap who "popped his clogs" was taking to the grave memories which formed a colourful part of our heritage.

At first I used Mr Pitman's shorthand. Then, buying a tape-recorder, I "did t'job proper". At first the dalesfolk I interviewed knew little or nothing about tape-recording. The same applied to me. I asked an old chap in Garsdale if I could "tape" him. He replied: "Tha can do what tha likes, lad." During the interview, he had some unkind things to say about the Forestry Commission. Afterwards, turning back the tape at random, I played over part of it, thinking he might be interested in hearing his own voice. From the tape recorder boomed his voice, denouncing the Forestry Commission. He stood up, excited, and said: "I telled thee I was right. Yon chap agrees with me!"

It was one of the Beresfords of Langstrothdale who told me about lively times at the George Inn, Hubberholme, when it was kept by Grace Pawson. Grace had an effective way of getting rid of unruly drinkers. Placing a poker in the fire, she waited until it was glowing red and brandished it near the offender. Two families teased Grace by going "on the spree" for six days and nights. The bar was kept open throughout with Grace presiding over it at night and her maid taking over during the day.

I picked up many a good tale while giving slide shows, which we offered free of charge. For almost fifty years, in many diverse places, I have extolled the beauty of the Yorkshire Dales and the characterfulness of the people. At first, I used one of the monster projectors with brass fittings and a bulb which ran so hot the projector was on the point of glowing. The slides were of the heavy glass variety. When the carrier was moved for the next slide there was a decided clonk.

Today, a slide show should be technically uneventful – but isn't. The other day, at a West Yorkshire town, I used the organiser's hi-tech projector with startling results. A slide jammed and was freed using tweezer's from a lady's manicure set. As I tried to free another slide, several shot out like "birds" at a clay pigeon shoot. One of them was "fielded" by the aforementioned lady. I lacerated my left thumb. A plaster offered by another member of the group staunched the blood. Working on the principle that the show must go on, and heaping displaced slides at the front of the projector stand, I filled in with humorous tales and wisecracks until the ordeal was over.

The chairlady thanked me for lifting the members' mid-winter gloom by wrestling with the projector as well as by what I had said. The secretary wrote: "Rather than prove to be a distraction, I think the antics of the projector added to the fun. I hope not many of your slides were damaged and that your thumb wasn't cut too badly."

Early Days

At our first meeting, in 1943, Harry Scott quoted Shakespeare, hailing me as "blithe spirit". It was my first morning in journalism. Harry made a breezy appearance in the reporter's room of the *Craven Herald* at mid-morning. He was just in time for coffee and one of Mr Bean's pork pies.

Harry was forty years old but looked middle-aged, with hair turning silvery, a face with loose-fitting skin and clothes so lacking in colour they verged on the drab. He fitted my image of a rural journalist perfectly. Harry had a ready smile, a quick wit, a way with words and a love affair with the printed word. During the lunch break, Harry rested his feet on a partly opened desk drawer and read books for pleasure. Or he would re-read copies of *John o' London's Weekly* a decade after they had been printed, glorying in their reflective prose and correct use of English.

All I knew about him when he suddenly appeared in the *Herald* office was that he had journeyed from a village called Clapham. Further inquiries revealed that in 1939, a few months before the outbreak of war, he had founded a monthly magazine called *The Yorkshire Dalesman*. When wartime conditions froze the circulation at 4,000, he took a part-time job at the *Herald* to augment the family income.

I had grown up at Skipton, gateway to the Yorkshire Dales. To the south, the landscape was industrialised. Northwards, for ninety and more miles, was unspoilt dale-country. The town was a blend of old and not-so-old. Memorials in the church and the ponderous gateway to Skipton Castle reminded me of the long tenure of the Cliffords. I grew up hearing so many tales about them I began to think of Lady Anne Clifford as a favourite aunt. I suppose I cried myself to sleep when somebody mentioned she'd been dead for several centuries.

Along the line of the Leeds and Liverpool canal were the back doors of mills. Smoke from a score of lanky chimneys smudged the grey northern sky. In my early years, the town was sharing the privations of a major industrial slump. The war followed. Tanks rumbled down the High Street. Among the Army officers based here was the handsome Richard Greene, film star, who in one production played the part of Robin Hood. At night, we heard the drone of enemy aircraft bound for Liverpool.

Eventually, a prisoner of war camp appeared beside the road to Bolton Abbey. Italians, then Germans, were quartered here and, on parole, might be seen walking about town in shabby battledress, with contrasting yellow or orange patches on the backs of their jackets. Food was rationed. The Americans sent us dried egg in cartons. When, during a break from work, I went home and made myself some tea, I used it to make an omelette and mixed it so stiffly it squeaked when pressed with a knife.

The Editor of the *Craven Herald*, John Mitchell, had employed me as a "cub" reporter at a time of staff shortage and also, I suspect, because of a family friendship with Mrs Hurst, whose brother, William Moss, Esq., was chairman of the directors. A dumpy Dickensian figure, Billy Moss wandered about town with a carpet bag and gave the impression, which he carefully cultivated, that he hadn't two pennies to rub together. In truth, he was bow-legged wi' brass. It had been customary for lads to pay for their training. I was the first to receive a wage – 12s.6d a week.

Harry was the first real journalist I had met. A man from a Quaker family, he did not quite fit into the mould of Hollywood reporters. He was – amiable. I never saw him lose his temper. He simply went tight-lipped and his face was a paler shade of grey. He had a puckish sense of humour and proved himself a poet when yet another outburst from the head printer with proofs to be read led him to pen some lines and paste them under the lid of his desk. They were:

What is that sound I hear so oft
Like wind among the willows;
Rising and falling and ever soft?
Hark, tis the burbling Billows.

As an ardent pipe-smoker, he scented the air with the fumes of a tobacco brand called Tom Long. As a former leader-writer on *The Yorkshire Post*, he wrote with a soft pencil. Our copy paper was nothing more than the outer layer of reels of newsprint battered during transit. Harry worked silently. Our archaic Olivetti, which he called a "tripewriter", resembled and sounded like a Lancashire loom.

The reporter's room, on the top floor of a rambling building, was spartan and careworn, with creaky floor, peeling walls and a pseudo-classical fireplace that in winter held a living fire. At other times of the year, there was the musty smell of old newsprint. Ancient files, brought out for research, showered pieces of brittle, yellowing paper over the floor covering of cracked lino.

I joined a reporting duo, Don and John Henry, and when we were not typing, we read proofs, incessantly, with one person holding the copy and the other, pencil poised over a galley of miniscule print, intoning like a high priest at some religious festival. None of us was hard-pressed in those days when paper rationing had shrunk the editorial content of the newspaper to relatively few columns of 6pt Monotype, which was marginally larger than the type found in a pocket diary.

Harry handed to us any difficult copy for re-typing. From my earliest days at the *Herald*, my eyes prickled with fatigue as I tried to read unreadable copy. I would be called on to disentangle (literally) the weekly report from the Misses Seed of Dent, who gave every item, even a report of a humble whist drive, a three-line heading, underlined in red, and who sewed sheets of copy together with large needle and bright red wool. Sam Stables, the Grassington correspondent was so annoyed when his news item about the sighting of an albino carrion crow was ignored, he shot the bird and posted the carcass to us with a short explanatory note. When the packet was opened, a small army of red mite re-grouped on the desk.

John Mitchell had a framed quotation on his wall: "Today is the tomorrow you worried about yesterday – and all is well". When reading proofs, he leaned back in his chair so that only two legs were touching the ground, and maintained a balance resting his feet on the desk. John was an unenthusiastic reader of proofs but an avid reader of Westerns. His nonchalant manner hid a man who had the welfare of young journalists at heart through his interest in pioneer training schemes. In my day, the job was learnt by trial and error.

Harry wrote leading articles, some of which reflected personal annoyances. For example, shortly after he received a rates demand, a leader appeared about the extravagance of local government. He also wrote a rag-bag feature, *A Craven Man's Diary*, using news cuttings about this and that. Each was given a topical introduction, which tended to be trite, an example being "A Craven man recently told me..." As the weeks went by, and more cuttings were used, that Craven man became quite a chatterbox.

Harry Scott (1903-1978), one of the best-known Yorkshiremen through his literary activity, was in truth a native of Hampshire. His family moved to Leeds when he was a child. Harry's first ambition on leaving a Quaker school in the West Riding was to become an architect, but so great was the cost of training the family persuaded him to take up accountancy. He joyfully left this profession for journalism, first with the *Yorkshire Evening News* and then with *The Yorkshire Post*.

He married Dorothy and they had two children, Margaret and Martin. Family holidays were spent in the Washburn Valley, where they rented part of a farm. The Scotts had no car. On working days, he would walk into Otley and catch a bus for Leeds. Now he planned to break away from daily journalism. He visited Robertson Scott, the founder of *The Countryman* at Burford in Oxfordshire, who proved to be autocratic. There would be precious little scope for advancement under him.

In 1935, Harry saw a newspaper advertisement for a "little house" to rent in Clapham. He took the family to see the place. They were entranced and moved here from Headingley. The agent of Ingleborough Estate had installed a new bath. Eddie Percy, of Settle, wired the premises for £14. For a time, Harry travelled daily by train into Leeds to continue working for *The Yorkshire Post*. He then left it for the uncertain world of freelance journalism. He hoped to earn £3 a week. His rent was 10s/50p a week and the cost of living negligible.

When in 1939 he launched *The Yorkshire Dalesman*, Harry had a clear vision of what he wanted to achieve. He benefited from advice given by his old friend, W L Andrews, autocratic editor of *The Yorkshire Post*. In 1939, he was one of six friends who each loaned him £50 to help him establish the magazine. It was Andrews who suggested that correspondence in *The Yorkshire Dalesman* should be presented not as "Letters to the Editor" but under the more chummy name of "Readers' Club".

Aware of the pulling power of famous names, Harry wrote to the Bishop of Bradford in 1939 asking for details of "a Dales experience". The Bishop, the celebrated Dr Blunt, whose hard words on royal infidelity had helped to precipitate the Abdication, replied: "Much as I like the Dale scenery, my knowledge of it is practically confined to motoring along its roads." He recommended that Harry should write to his registrar, Mr F A T Mossman, adding: "He appears to have walked the whole of the Dale country... He certainly knows all about the inns."

In 1940, Harry was corresponding with Arthur Raistrick, the Dales historian, who had found his pacifist position difficult to maintain with fairness to his college at Newcastle-upon-Tyne. He had secured leave of absence until the end of the war. "This is without pay, so we hope to experiment in simple living."

Kit Calvert, who in the 1930s had been hailed as the saviour of the cheese-making industry at Hawes, wrote asking if "Professor Raistrick" might suggest a value for a book he had just picked up for £2. "I think it must be worth more than that." The tome was John Ogilby's *Britannia or The Kingdom of England and the Dominion of Wales*, published in 1698 and containing a hundred maps "same as those you recently published in the *Dalesman*."

The Clapham house was in a part of the village known as Gildersbank. Harry got permission to change the name to Fellside. The first choice had been Beckside, from its relation to Fell Beck. He took over the front parlour where the magazine's 28 pages of material and outside cover were prepared, to be hand-set and printed by Lamberts of Settle. The first issue of 3,000 copies cost £25 and was retailed at thruppence.

Fellside, Clapham

Life at Clapham

In 1948, after two years national service in the Royal Navy, I returned to "civvy street" to receive a letter from Harry Scott, who invited me to visit him at Clapham. "There are a number of possibilities we might then talk over." A previous letter had updated me about his Dales magazine. "Our sales are now 13,000 a month...and our books go well. We have a considerable number of new books planned for 1948."

An orange-sided *Pennine* bus, with Lile Jackie at the wheel, delivered me to Clapham, via Buckhaw Brow. The bus, one of a valiant little fleet which invested every trip with a dash of adventure, had been given its distinctive colour when the proprietors visited Leyland in

Lancashire to buy their first vehicle in the 1920s. They chose orange, as used for the bus that took the Leyland football team to their fixtures.

I was about to become 50% of the editorial staff of *The Dalesman*. The landscape brightened at the approach of Settle, the brown gritstone giving way at the fault-line to pearl-white limestone. Here was a magical land of waterfalls and caves. At Settle, I saw my first potholer, a young man intent on exploring an underworld of potholes and caves. At least, I presumed it was a potholer. He clambered on to the bus at Settle with a coil of rope ladder and sat in front of an old lady, who asked, with a Dales curiosity coupled with a measure of cheek: "Are you one o' these pothoiler chaps?" He nodded. The old lady reflected, then said: "Nay, lad – doesn't ta think tha'll spend enuff time under t'ground wi'out going there now?"

In the market place at Settle, I stared with disbelief at *Ye Olde Naked Man*, an inn which was now a café. I was told of an old saying, "Anything will clothe a naked man". So anyone who was faddy [fastidious] about food "mun be ready to eat owt – a poorly hoss or a scabby monkey." A tall, shabbily-dressed man was Old Mick, the bull-walloper [cattle drover], emerging from the *Royal Oak*, where people regularly challenged him to drink twelve pints to twelve strokes of the clock and provided the ale for him to attempt the feat. An old injury meant he no longer gulped while drinking. Ale went down his throat like water down a drain. Mick never managed to "down" 12 pints at a time, but he thoroughly enjoyed the challenge.

As the bus ground its way up Buckhaw Brow, then descended Cave Ha', the driver, Jackie, had his breakfast. He kept the bus on the road by grasping the steering wheel with his right hand while his left hand groped for, located and delivered to his mouth the bacon butties in which he called his bait-bag. The bus roared on to Austwick.

Now the skyline was crowned by a flat-topped hill, part of a group of fells that sprawled languidly, giving the impression of a lion at rest. Distance and cloud shadow gave the hill a blue-grey tone. An old farmer remarked: "That's Ingleborough...It's a big rough hill. And wild! The wind's strong enuff to blaw a sheep ower. I wouldn't be capped [surprised] to see snow up yon on Midsummer Day." The farmer was in his best setting-off suit, plus nebbed cap and brown leggings.

At Clapham, Lile Jackie coaxed the bus round a blind corner and over a hump-backed bridge. He drew up outside the post office. The welcoming party was a hungry swan, which should have been admiring its reflection while cruising on Ingleborough Lake. Instead, it found easy pickings in the village and amused itself by terrorising old ladies. Its mate had been knocked down on the bridge. It perished under the wheels of a lorry from Leeds. The driver picked up the substantial body and hurled it over the parapet, commenting to an amazed onlooker: "It's nobbut a duck."

In pre-bypass days, all traffic ground its way through the village. A large vehicle with a cargo of tinned food, then subject to rationing, had failed to negotiate the New Inn corner and descended into the beck, just below the big waterfall. What had been for centuries a quiet, law-abiding community became one of wreckers. Every house – even that of the constable who was in bed with sciatica – had its share of booty. There was one snag. The water had washed away the labels. No one could be quite sure, when they prepared a meal, what would feature in the main course. Sometimes, it was fruit.

Nearly everyone had a story of someone (never the narrator) who had benefited from the wartime black market. At a pub near Giggleswick, ham and eggs never went off the menu the war through. The flitches were stored in a loft, under the slates, and a railwayman who lodged there used to go up in summer and scrape off the maggots. I heard of the farmer who was driving a vanload of black market meat when he saw a police cordon. He did not stop. His wife said: "Tha's done it this time. They're bound to have got t'cars number." Her husband told her not to worry about it. "Just afore I set off from home, I covered t'number plates wi' cow muck."

And there was the Settle decorator who returned to town with his van groaning under meat from friendly farmers. A policeman stopped him near Settle Bridge. What had he got in the van? The joiner told him precisely what he had. The policeman said: "That's last time I'm going to let you pull my leg. Off you go!"

Clapham looked old but was in truth a 19th century village. The old Clapham was re-styled by the Farrer family. The body of the church was rebuilt and soon bedecked by Farrer memorials. They lived in style at Ingleborough Hall, contriving by making a series of tunnels for tradesfolk and others to reach the back door of the hall without being seen from the front. Two tunnels also enabled them to extend the grounds over an old lane so the family might be driven to a limestone grotto in woodland without entering the village proper.

They put a stone and earth plug in Clapdale and made a lake where they might fish and from which was piped the local water supply. Water also activiated a turbine, generating electric power for several important houses and also for street lighting.

In the immediate post-war period, Ingleborough Hall, their old home, had been sold, to become a special school owned by the West

Riding County Council. Here, children suffering from asthmatic and bronchial problems responded to fresh air, exercise and wholesome food. Claude Barton, the agent, and his family lived at imposing Hall Garth. New families, under trial as workers on Ingleborough estate, had been initially housed in the old toll house, a mile from Clapham, and if they behaved themselves were re-housed in a cottage. My first lodging, with the Shaws at the woodyard, was the nearest place to the water turbine. A huge electrical dial was fixed to a living room wall. At an appointed time, an electric switch was thrown and, lo, there was light!

Fell Beck flowed powerfully through the village, dividing it into two and making it necessary to have numerous bridges, one of them called t'Brokken Bridge. This was the one I crossed to reach the home of the Scotts. I paused on the bridge. The local dipper, a podgy dark bird with a white "bib", was doing its morning press-ups on a water-washed stone. A kingfisher flew by, quick and direct, like a blue dart. A neighbour of the Scotts was Sam West, postman, who came into his own on Remembrance Sunday when, wearing an astrakhan coat, he led the British Legion members to the war memorial.

The home of the Scotts had its façade covered by Virginia creeper, a nesting place for a pair of spotted flycatchers and a dormitory, in the off-season, for chirruping sparrows. A slated garden path lay between sheep-nibbled wallflowers and led to the main door. A pile of parcels, containing the latest issue of *The Yorkshire Dalesman*, flanked a central passage. Dorothy Scott had covered the unsightly stack with a cloth on which reposed a vase of flowers.

There was a small dining room where the morning routine began with the opening of mail amid the marmalade and toast. Beyond, in what was intended to be a lounge, stood a huge desk and four-drawer filing cabinet. The walls were lagged with books. The office was heated by a coke stove. Harry's chair stood immediately in front of it and he developed a system of slipping pieces of cardboard between himself and the stove – a simple but effective way of controlling the heat.

Harry used the big desk. I was relegated to a small desk in a corner where, in dull conditions, I might switch on a light from an unshielded bulb in a fitting attached to the wall. One of my jobs was to take any subscriptions received in the morning mail to the bus for Bentham, where they would receive the attention of Elsie Dickinson, our clerk.

At the time of which I am thinking, the cost of an annual postal subscription to the magazine was 10s.6d. What Harry Scott could do that day depended largely on how many postal orders were received. At least, postal subscribers to the magazine paid in advance. Harry told me that when the magazine was first published, all the relevant documents were kept in a boot box.

The Dalesman already had its folklore. Harry was fond of relating when Professor Joad, of BBC Brains Trust fame, appeared sopping wet on the doorstep after climbing Ingleborough and was allowed to have a bath while his clothes were dried. A year later, as will be related, the artist Ionicus descended from those self-same heights, where he had been seeking caves to draw for a feature that would appear in *Punch*. He did not find his caves and we provided him with photographs of the underworld on which he might base his work. Subsequently, for 16 years, he provided us with cover illustrations.

Autumn brought the russet flare of discoloured leaves on the creeper that spread over most of the façade of the *Dalesman* home. Winter saw the arrival of a load of logs for the fire and mountain sheep intent on stripping the garden of its wallflowers. The spotted flycatchers returned to nest in spring, by which time the village seemed to echo with bird song and long-nebbed curlews flew high and uttered their bubbling calls.

With an hourly service, the bus stop was a place where I met some fascinating characters. Ben Hudson, a farmer, had a short, sharp form of speech and didn't like to waste words. His wife Dora usually did his talking for him. One day, as we waited for the bus to arrive, Dora mentioned that they were going on holiday to Morecambe, adding: "We'll only be there ten minutes when Ben'll be asking t'way to Lancaster auction mart." Arthur Tennant, of Bull and Cave Farm – a name relating to an old inn name – was a devout Methodist who would not say "Hello" because it was "O Hell", the wrong way round.

Mr Brown, the sub-postmaster, was an enterprising man. He told me he could sell anything, if he set his mind to it, even "gravel in fancy bags." Mr Murray, the gamekeeper, told me of going the round of the farms to purchase broody hens for incubating pheasant eggs. At breeding time, he would clamber out of his bed at two or three in the morning and be still working until ten at night. I heard of Old Douglas, the woodman, who worked for the estate for 40 years and planted many of the trees.

In the early days, I lodged. After work, I would follow the broad carriageway through the woods, beside the lake and out to where the mouth of Ingleborough Cave gave the impression that a limestone cliff was yawning. Arnold Brown, the cave guide, carrying a paraffin lamb, would lead me underground, having handed me a candle-holder with three prongs. On our way towards the heart of Ingleborough, we passed calcite formations. One imposing stalactite was known as the Sword of Damocles.

Near the end of the show cave, Cave Man Brown stopped at an array of stalactites and tapped them with the key to the cave, producing a bell-like sound. Harry Harrison, his predecessor as guide, had waited until he literally had a captive audience, far from daylight, when he dowsed some of the lights and offered some of his poetry for sale.

The spirit of the Farrers still brooded over Clapham in my early days with *Dalesman*. A hostelry near Clapham railway station was named after their crest, the flying horse-shoe. Still well remembered were James Anson Farrer (1849-1923) and his wife Elizabeth, the former Miss Reynell-Pack, who had family connections with the Sitwells. The Farrers had two sons, Reginald John, who became internationally famous as a plant-collector, artist and writer but was only forty when he died in the wilds of Upper Burma, and Sydney James, who married

Violet Maud Monkton. Sydney spent his life in the shadow of his illustrious brother. Violet stayed in nobody's shadow and attained the local status of an "angel", being indefatigable in her charitable and church works.

When I lodged with Jack Winton and his family, and helped him restore the Reginald Farrer rock garden to tidiness, if not to its original splendid condition, I had time to ponder on the achievements of this astonishing man. He was born with physical disabilities, including hair-lip and cleft palate. Gossipy letters I received from the Hon Mrs R Wood, of St George's Square, London, gave me an insight into Reginald's life and attitudes. As young Marion, the daughter of a close friend of Mrs Farrer, she happily related details of visits to Ingleborough Hall. I wrote back, stating I would not mention her name. She replied: "It is of no consequence. I haven't met a Farrer for at least 60 years".

She had often stayed at Ingleborough Hall and was exactly 10 years younger than Reginald. "When I was a child, about six or seven years old, my mother – knowing I should see Reginald while my parents and Mr and Mrs Farrer were off at Cannes – explained to me that Reginald could not talk normally. I mustn't show any surprise or it would hurt his feelings. I was rather a precocious little thing and duly took Reginald's queer voice and looks without showing I had noticed anything." Mrs Farrer herself told Marion that only she could understand what he said until he was well into his teens.

Marion "really knew Reginald very well. He was very kindly – an elder brother to me!…It wasn't true, as many people said, that he was conceited. He wasn't. He was merely trying – oh! so hard –to hide the fact that he minded his disability terribly." One story illustrated Reginald's great love for his mother, who had shown such consideration during his difficult upbringing. "With the very first money which Reginald earned as a writer – when he was in his twenties – he bought a necklace and gave it to his mother."

The ruling Farrer in the earliest days of my Clapham vocation was

Matthew Roland (1886-1952), who when he took over the family estate on the death of his brother had been a sheep farmer in New Zealand. Claude Barton (normally called Bill by his family and friends) was completing a long tenure of the estate agent's office.

There had been only one major new building in Clapham over the past half century and that was the hanger-like garage beside the main road. Mr Barton put the work in hand. It is said that when he asked James Anson Farrer if he might build a garage, Farrer was thinking he wanted somewhere to house his private car. As usual, Farrer left it to his agent to sort things out. When the Farrers returned to the village after an absence of several weeks, they were astonished to find the huge single-span building with its hexagonal cross-beams. It was visible from Ingleborough Hall. Farrer insisted that a row of trees should be planted as a screen.

Bert Cross, born in 1909, who started work there in about 1926, remembered when the commonest types of private vehicle on the road were the Model T Ford and the bull-nosed Morris. One of the Fords ran over the cliff into the beck and was found to be still on its wheels in the middle of the watercourse. Bert remembered the grand days when the Farrers went as guests to Underley Hall, travelling in a horse-drawn carriage. The horses, which were not permitted to walk between the two places, completed the journey in an hour.

The main road was given a tarred surface about 1923. As a lad, Bert used to stand by the road in dry weather and watch motor bikes disappear in a cloud of dust. Dr Lovett, a Scot who was the local medical practitioner, had a motor bike which he used periodically to reach Meets at Gaping Gill on the flanks of Ingleborough. He was fond of walking, took young people from Clapham into the country, invariably lit a fire and coaxed it into life by blowing down his stethoscope.

When Bert Cross left school, one of his jobs was to keep his cars in good order in case the doctor was called out at night. He provided new carbide for the lighting system. This was how Bert got a job working for Mr Barton at the garage. In the early 1930s, Bert sometimes drove an ex-laundry van, a Garforth, which had solid tyres on the back wheels. It was used to cart coal and coke from Clapham station to Lawkland Hall, Newby Cote and other grand houses in the district.

The coal was shovelled into the van through holes cut in the sides. Said Bert: "I used to take the shooters up to the moors in this old Garforth. I then carted the beaters. We covered the holes with celluloid curtains to keep the bad weather out." An Austwick man who rented an adjacent moor for grouse-shooting arranged for food, mainly beef and bread, to be transported for the beaters. One year, the bread was overlooked. "We had sandwiches, just t'same – two pieces o' lean beef wi' some fat in t'middle."

Until the coming of Dickie Lamb's bus service, anyone going to Settle had at least three miles to walk – from Clapham to the railway station and from Giggleswick railway station into town. The bus services and trains on branch lines soon to be closed provided me with the means of travel when first I ventured forth to meet and record the memories of folk in the Yorkshire Dales during what would turn out to be a social revolution.

On my first jaunt, into upper Wharfedale, I waved at a farm man who cycled by wearing a back-can with milk drawn from the cattle lodged at an outbarn. A roadman was using a sickle to trim the road verges. I operated by Dales time. A villager, asked when a neighbour had died, thought hard for a while, then replied: "If she'd lived till tomorrow, she'd have been dead a fortnight." It seems that the death occurred at a whist drive. "It was all very sad – she had a good hand."

After years during which the magazine was hand-set by Messrs Lambert at the Caxton Press, Settle, we went to Dixon and Stell of Cross Hills, thence to Messrs Atkinson and Pollitt of Kendal. Most days there was editorial work to be done and then we engaged in a campaign for new advertising or the production of a book.

A round of letters ensured we had a supply of review copies of books. Harry was a voracious reader, spending most of his evenings by the fireside, engrossed in the latest works. We sent out thousands of specimen copies of the magazine, intent on getting new subscribers. Harry's special ambition was to get a copy of the magazine into the waiting room of every dentist in the land.

From a deep window on the landing of the house, one might survey the back garden, with its high wall, which kept it snug when a wind was rampaging from the cold quarters. Dorothy Scott laboured hard and long and here, on those old-fashioned sunny days, the family relaxed. In wartime, the garden had housed a pig that helped the Scotts to supplement the meagre food rations, though this batch of pork had poor keeping qualities. The butcher added: "It must have got het up. Tha must keep a pig calm on its last day."

I was responsible for the early demise of a fish and chip project organised by the butcher's wife, in the premises also used by her husband. She provided me with fish and chips free of charge, having hinted that I might write a "puff par" about her enterprise for the *Craven Herald*. Many people read the piece, including an official of the district council who insisted on the cooking area being tiled out and washing facilities provided, a costly matter. Her husband was upset at the loss of income. He drank rather a lot at the *New Inn* and periodically was seen standing on the bridge, staring moodily at the water, as though wondering whether or not to jump. For a week or two I avoided eye contact.

In time, even the patient and kind-hearted Dorothy Scott felt that the office should be moved so she might recover her sitting room. Ingleborough Estate, which had provided the "little house" now made available for sale some old workshops "up t'ginnel". They were extensively altered. The old "sawpit" was filled in. A hand-operated estate fire-fighting appliance was trundled away.

Eddie Gower, the advert manager, was to remember with amusement to his dying day the transfer of *Dalesman* furnishings and files to the new premises, which lay across t'beck. Eddie borrowed a handcart from the estate and, with my help, piled it with paper and the less substantial items of office equipment. Down from the gate at Fellside, a gust of wind created a shower of displaced papers and dropped most of them in the beck. We retrieved some, but – as Eddie put it – "possible masterpieces of literature were wafted under the bridge, over the waterfall and were waterborne to the river Wenning."

Dick Clark, a retired railway signalman, who had daily commuted by bike from Clapham to Helwith Bridge, became part-time handyman at our offices. He was a real character – chubby, friendly and with a distinctive way of looking at life. He attended to a coke-fired boiler. He took mail to the post office and he made tea, which he delivered to the various offices. Eddie recalled how, when he brought the afternoon tea, two cups on a tray, he would sometimes remark: "Let's see – one of these is sweetened." He took a noisy sip from one cup and said: "It's the other one", handing the tasted cup to Eddie. I would get the other cup – along with a chocolate-coated biscuit, which he drew, in its naked form, from the cavernous depths of a pocket in his thick, blue serge trousers.

The vicar at the time had a large garden, adjacent to our new office block. He was not in good health and abhorred gardening. We were able to buy most of it and also half of a huge barn. We got the half in which a vicar of old kept his horse and trap. It became the editorial department. What for a time was like a secluded monastery garden, flanked by high walls, soon had a wall breeched and became a car park.

It was here, on a never-to-be-forgotten afternoon that a brass band from Tasmania played some rousing tunes. Many copies of the *Dalesman* were posted to what had been parts of the British Empire, the home of immigrants from Yorkshire. A reader who was connected with the brass band at Hobart arranged that during a British tour they would call at Clapham and play on condition that afterwards they were served with cups of good strong Yorkshire tea and iced buns. The condition was met. I received a tie decorated with a kangeroo. I complained because it did not have a pouch.

Dalesfolk at Home

There was no transport department at *The Dalesman*. Harry Scott's driving career had been brief. The last car he owned had such a fickle engine that once started it was unwise to stop it except within pushing distance of a garage. If the family went to Skipton to shop, they would tour the shops while he stood by the car, ensuring that the engine kept running. In my time, he occasionally took the train to Leeds, trudging one and a-half miles to the station, alert at all times for the drove of semi-wild horses which then roamed Newby Moor.

At the sound of clattering hooves, it was wise for a pedestrian to nip over the nearest wall. Occasionally, the unruly horses bore down on the green at Newby. They perished, one by one, under the wheels of vehicles crossing the moor. How could the driver of the Pennine bus, with the faint headlights of the time, expect to see a black horse on a dark night?

Dorothy Scott went to Settle market by bus. When there had been a good week for 10s.6d postal orders, we might arrange to travel to an appointment using Tommy Hargreaves's taxi. Tommy's lorries, like the horses, impinged on Newby green, and consequently the village had little chance of winning one of the beauty contests which were organised at the time by the *News Chronicle*. One year, Linton received the main award, which the organisers called art but some ruralists thought of as expensive litter.

For my first excursions into the Dales I combined public transport with Shanks pony. It was not a hardship to "leg it". While working at the *Craven Herald* in 1944, I had attended the funeral of C J Cutcliffe Hyne at Kettlewell, using the bus as far as Grassington and walking the rest of the way. An old chap who had a lively tread, though he was well into his eighties, remarked: "Ay, lad - when this pace stops, I stops." Something must have overtaken me on that long, long road to Kettlewell but I cannot recall it. It was enough to be walking on a warm, calm day, which was sunny when nature had blinked the sleep mist from her eyes.

In the 1950s, many of the farmers could not afford to run a car. Their presence on a bus gave it an earthy smell at muck-spreading time. If it

wasn't the tang of muck that pervaded the bus, there was the acrid fumes from half a dozen tobacco pipes to taint the air. Dr Pickles of Aysgarth, one of the best-known doctors in the Dales, studied the effect the bus service had on the spread of infectious diseases.

Most of the dalesfolk were at home for most of the time, which was handy for me when I had interviews in mind. In the autumn of 1952, I made what I considered to be an adventurous journey into Swaledale. I stayed there for several days, during which there was an alternation of sunshine and shower. The sky was washed hourly. Kisdon, the "island hill", rimmed by purple heather, stood out with the clarity of operatic scenery.

I took "pot luck", calling without appointment, an old Dales custom. I was usually lucky with regard to the pot. I soon discovered it was unwise to go to the front door of a farm, which had not been opened for years and around which was stuffed a draught-proof barrier of old sacks. Or if it was used, it was of the type protected from wind and rain by a porch. In this case, there was a passage beyond, on one wall of which hung a barometer. When one of these was set "fair" and, outside, the elements were wild, the farmer took the barometer from the wall into the garden, held it up and said: "Sitha!"

A typical house had a living kitchen which was grey-flagged, the chill taken away by pegged rugs. The furniture was usually of deal, being cheap to buy and scrubbable. If there was a big family, the table was flanked by wooden forms, with a chair at either end. A cane chair stood near the fire. In farmhouses, it was often draped by a fleece, usually a black 'un, which had not been included when the wool-clip was sold. The most valuable item of furniture would be a longcase clock, made within a few miles of where it had stood throughout its long life.

The central feature of one wall, and rising almost to the ceiling, was a range, kept shiny by weekly applications of black lead. The fireplace was flanked by oven and hot-water boiler. On either side of the high mantelpiece were pot dogs, behind which reposed documents awaiting attention and reminders of action to be taken. A Dales kettle crooned to itself on a stand beside the coal fire, which was central feature of a huge range shiny from an application of black lead. The Dalesfolk liked their tea well "mashed" and piping hot, though one old lady, delivering a cup of tea to her husband, said: "I've stirred it and blowed it." Slurping from a saucer demanded some concentration.

Mrs Parker, at the Post Office, had lived in Muker since 1912 but was still regarded by the auld folk as a Gunnersider. Her late husband Tom had delivered mail to Tan Hill Inn, cycling 16 miles a day. He took his lunch with him and waited at Tan Hill until the residents had dealt with their correspondence and jotted down any replies. Nanny Peacock, who kept the only inn at Muker, selling ale at 1 1/2d a glass, was once asked if she ever went to Chapel. Nanny replied: "No. Ah doesn't – but Ah respect those 'at does."

I heard that Dick Guy, whose home was near the bridge at Muker, started the first bus service in the dale in 1920. He used an old Seabrook lorry, a flat-bodied vehicle on which rows of seats were fitted. The seats came from an old four-in-hand horse 'bus. The passengers sat in the open. The service consisted of a return trip to Richmond on market day.

It was Dick who told me the story of an ancient dalesman who took to his death-bed. Neighbours and friends visited the house and sat up with him at night, for the man was weary and restless and needed companionship. When Mary Anne's turn came round, she went to his bedroom, saw the old chap was comfortable and decided to snatch some sleep. She lay on a couch and draped a rug across her body. Mary Anne was just ready to doze off when the old chap called out: "Mary, is thoo sittin' up wi' me, or is Ah sittin' up wi' thee?"

I walked from Muker to Gunnerside, along the little-used road. It was a splendid vantage point. The village was revealed in its linear form between alluvial land, almost as flat and finely green as a billiards table, and a fellside scarred where stone had been wrenched from living beds and t'auld man, while probing for galena, had tormented the landscape.

Gunnerside still had traces of its old-time independence. There was a cobbler known affectionately as John Robert who not only made boots but provided an informal while-you-wait service. The rasp of clog-irons against gravel was a common sound in those pre-welly days. I also saw a smithy, owned by the Calvert family. Willie Calvert loved to tell of the Horse Age, and especially of that day in 1950 when he and his son shod 14 horses. "We were working till midnight." Willie had grown up in a village with a strong lead-mining connection. The anvil in the smithy rested on a roller from a mine. He had heard tales of miners who looked ancient at fifty from working in cramped, damp places. In some mines, the air was so foul a candle would not burn. The so-called gruver's complaint was a form of silicosis.

Ruth Alderson told me her uncles were lead miners. "Many of the men never saw the village in daylight when winter came along – except on Sunday...Some of the mines were three miles away, in diffi-cult country. There were no clocks to watch up there." When Ruth Alderson's father, George, took up a job as watcher at an Engine House, he had two miles to travel underground to get to his work. Sir George Dennis, a mine owner, gave each of the women who worked at the washings a flannel petticoat as a Christmas present. When Sir George came to Gunnerside, he was met by t'brass band who played his favourite tune – *The Girl I left behind Me*.

Having heard so much about lead-mining, I lingered at Low Row to have a chat with the novelist Thomas Armstrong, who lived at Lawn House. His book *Adam Brunskill*, one of a series of books which had become best-sellers, was based on much local research into the local quest for lead. Thomas Armstrong was a handsome man, with snow-white hair and an affable manner. He had a passion for cricket and also for practical work, such as re-designing his garden using lots of local stone. He usually had a pipe in his mouth.

I chatted with him in the drawing room at Lawn House, partly lagged with books on shelves and decorated by Dales water-colours, the work of Wensleydale artist Fred Lawson. Thomas Armstrong had found that Swaledale folk are slow to accept a stranger. "They weigh you up carefully. If you get through twelve months and they decide you are all right, you become one of them." This was the time-hon-oured Dales process of "wintering and summering and wintering again."

I inquired about the physically as well as mentally-demanding task of gathering material for Adam Brunskill, his great lead-mining novel. His best sources had been diaries belonging to miners or mine agents. In eighteen months of research, he gathered 500,000 words in reference notes for a novel that had a length of 260,000 words. At a time when many modern novels included characters who talked and amused themselves but apparently had no job of work, Thomas Armstrong had clearly made sure his characters had plenty to do.

At Low Row I sauntered into the workshop of Ernest Bagshaw, joiner and undertaker. We did not get round to discussing the celebrated Corpse Road, which traversed the dale, and along which the bodies of daleheaders who had died were borne to the nearest consecrated ground, which was at Grinton. Death held no terrors for these faithful dalesfolk and everyone loved a funeral tale, such as that about the Methodist minister who spoke so effusively about the man whose body lay in the coffin before him that the hitherto grieving widow looked concerned. Turning to her son, she said: "Tha'd better go and open up yon coffin. I think they've got t'wrong chap."

Ernest began his reminiscences in the pre-motor age, when at the first hint of a death in the dale he would alert the owners of three pairs of black horses. One pair would be required to draw the hearse. Victorian grief had a public expression. Families who had spare "brass" ordered black-edged funeral cards which bore brief details of the "dear departed". Funeral cakes were distributed to relatives and friends. These cakes were of a type that was cut across the middle, folded, wrapped in good quality white paper and sealed with black wax.

Before the mourners left the home of the deceased, they were provided with a dinner including ham and beef. Wine, either port or sherry, was served before the funeral. After the hearse came the mourning coaches, black landaux and the farm folk with their horses and traps. Anyone who called at a house where someone had died was invited to view the corpse in the coffin. One visitor said to a widow: "I do believe he's smiling." Replied the widow: "Aye, lass – he doesn't knaw he's deeard yet!"

Down at Richmond, they told the tale of the new milk-lad who thought he would drum up some extra trade for his employer. He began knocking on doors at random. One door was opened by a young lady. She asked: "Do you want to see mi dad?" "Aye". She took him upstairs, where dad, newly-dead, was lying in his coffin.

On those days of long ago when I walked down Swaledale, I arrived in Reeth on a day when sunshine gave the area a technicoloured splendour. Reeth, at the junction of Swaledale and Arkengarthdale, was a good vantage point for the ruler-straight Fremington Edge. There was time, that evening, to cross the bridge, walk through several fields, passing an outbarn and climbing near the White House to reach the moorland rim, where I listened for a while to the grouse chatting with gutteral voices.

Fremington Edge was the proverbial scene of activity as workmen secured blocks of chert. This was quarrying, even though it took place in underground chambers. The tools used by the men were as employed in local quarries and would have been inappropriate in lead-mines. In 1941, Frank Woodall, of Shipley, was hereabouts, on a day's excursion from Redmire, where he was staying. He packed some photographic equipment for a walk on Fremington Edge.

Frank saw a crane at the roadside and was told about the chert quarry. The men were having their snack and playing halfpenny nap. One of them, a Cornishman, had arrived at Hurst, above Swaledale, in 1918 to take part in a lead-mining venture that failed. Frank was invited to go underground. "Now this is the strange thing," he told me. "It was a brilliant sunny day but for some unknown reason I had packed a tin of photographic flash-powder and so was able to take some photographs underground."

Robert Gill, of Reeth, was the first of his family in six centuries who had not been associated with lead-mining in Arkengarthdale. He said that a miner needed good legs – and a walking stick, unless he was one of those living at Healaugh and Reeth who worked the mines of Preston-under-Scar. They knitted while walking to and from work to augment the family income. A man with a huge pack visited the area to distribute more wool and collect the finished items. Some men wore long stockings because they reduced "drag" in the confined spaces of a lead mine.

In my early days with *The Dalesman*, I concentrated on Wharfedale. At Hubberholme, a farm man cycled by with a can of milk on his back. The back-can, with its special harness, was said to be of two types – uphill and downhill. I thought this was yet another example of Dales leg-pulling until it was pointed out that a lighter can was needed if the outbarns, where milking took place, were lower than the farmstead where the milk was to be dealt with. It was said, in days when people were not obsessed by hygene, that "milk tastes o' nowt unless t'cow's had its foot in t'bucket."

With my elbows resting on the parapet of the bridge, I listened to the song of the Wharfe – a pleasant song that day, when the river was little more than a trickle. At flood-time, it was known to overflow the banks. The little church at Hubberholme had been flooded to such a depth that fish were found swimming between the pews. Or so "they" say.

The vicar, Harry Isherwood, recalled standing on the bridge with

Colin Wills, a broadcaster. When Mr Isherwood had related how the turbulent Wharfe had upset the fabric of the church, the microphone was held so that wireless listeners might hear the sound of the river. Thousands of miles away, in Hong Kong, a member of the Falshaw family, who was in the Army, had the heart-stirring experience of hearing the river of his native district at a distance of thousands of miles. Mrs Isherwood taught at Oughtershaw School. Among the names on the register were those of children living at remote Cam Houses. She had a picture of the Good Shepherd. A small girl, one of a farming family, said: "It's a funny thing, miss, but all those sheep in the picture are half-bred."

Fred Falshaw, of Buckden, was the Poo-bah of Upper Wharfedale - postman, milkman, butter factor, butcher and hawker. The butter, produced at the farms, was retailed in summer for as little as sixpence a pound. Some families supplied a grocer with butter, bartering it for groceries. If Fred could not sell his butter he retained it to make salve, a mixture of fat and tar that was applied to the skins of sheep in the autumn.

It was Fred who told me that about the turn of the century tradesmen from Wensleydale had visited Buckden with oatmeal, which was sold at about 1s a stone. "It *was* oatmeal. You could smell it half a mile off!" Fred hawked Yarmouth Bloaters, which were salted herrings, cured at Richmond by James Bell. Fred bought them at Leyburn market for 5d a box, which contained a dozen, sometimes one or two more. "I was butchering for a while. I killed my own sheep and bought beef from a wholesale butcher in Burnley. T'best cuts were about 6d. It was nowt fresh for a family to buy a lump of 20 pounds at a slap. A lot of t'farmers had beef two or three times a day. And every farmer fed two or three pigs..."

At Kettlewell, I had the company of Kit Wiseman, a member of a family who over several generations had been carriers in the dale, one of their jobs being transporting coal in hefty two-wheeled "block" carts. John Raw and his sons made these carts at Kettlewell. A "decent" cart cost between £10 and £12. Benjamin Ward, a local blacksmith, hooped the wheels with iron. Benjamin had been in business long enough to remember fitting simple shoes to cows that were about to be driven on long journeys.

When Kit came of working age, his father did not encourage him to "lig" in bed. At 3 a.m., he was up and about, feeding the horses. "By

Grassington.

five o' clock, we'd be leaving Kettlewell on business. Day was almost gone when we got back home again." On his travels in Wharfedale, he often came across drovers with sheep or cattle. Richard Thwaite, who lived in Bishopdale, believed in being comfortable when he was droving. He either rode a pony or travelled by gig.

Kit could just remember when the first mowing machine reached Kettlewell. "Before that time, the grass was mown by long-pole scythe. There'd be a team of men working together. My uncle stood 6ft-odd in his stockinged feet and his scythe blade came up to his chin. He could cut a swathe three yards wide and a yard forrard."

My next long excursion was to North Ribblesdale, where – a few years after the 1939-45 war – the Settle-Carlisle railway looked careworn, having been flogged hard, with only essential repairs. At the time I first became interested in the railway, it had not become celebrated but was simply another line, used by soot-streaked locomotives and their rakes of carriages or wagons.

A farmer who was leuking [looking] sheep said: "They do tell me that yon viaduct was built on wool." I believed him until detailed research was to reveal that each pier stood on bedrock over which lay a coverlet of concrete – repeat, concrete. "Aye," continued the farmer, "there were a chap crossing yon viaduct on a windy day who lost his cap. It was blown ower one o' t'parapets." He paused, for effect. "Aye – t'wind blew it under one of t'arches, up t'other side, ower t'other parapet, right on to his 'eeard. He complained afterwards. It was t'wrong way round. The neb were at t'back!" There was a wheezy sound, like that of a rusty gate moving on its hinges. The farmer was laughing.

In those days, the stationmaster was Martin Elliott. He ran a station, with an adjacent quarry that produced 1,000 tons of ground limestone a week. The limestone contained up to 99 per cent of calcium carbonate. Once an hour, Martin reported on the state of the weather in a

coded message telephoned to the Air Ministry weather station at Dunstable. He told me that a hundred trains a day used the Settle-Carlisle. Later, standing near a cave mouth from which water issued, I had the company of the roadman. He told me of the "navvies" who built the line. Navvy is a general term for a score of specialist occupations. For example, Welsh masons positioned the limestone blocks of which the immense viaduct was made.

The roadman's grandparents had come to Ribblehead when the line was being built in the 1870s. He had a plain wooden desk from which the navvies had been paid. He told me that the temperature in the huts on summer days was so high that candles and butter and other meltable commodities were stored in the cave near which we were standing.

In the late 1940s, the fells were being gripped [mechanically drained]. On the tawny ground on either side of the valley were dark lines, in patterns, resembling a giant spider's web. And, like a web, they were lifeless. Hill country which had acted like a sponge, absorbing rainfall and releasing it gradually, was now being rapidly eroded. Storm water found the grips and deepened them, at the same time discolouring the becks and rivers and bringing the rivers into rapid spate and floods breaking out more often in the lowlands.

The so-called Town Hall, at Selside, was deteriorating. Originally a dwelling, the building converted into an institute where local folk might gather on winter evenings to play cards in a windowless space that was heated by a coal fire. With the outbreak of the 1939-45 war, there was no coal allocation for t'Town Hall and many young men had joined the Forces. Mrs Sunter, who attended the Queen's jubilee celebrations at Horton in 1887 was amused when Squire Foster produced a bowl containing syrup. Into the bowl he dropped two half-crowns. Men were invited to recover the money with their teeth. A man who, henceforth, was known as Treacle Billy won the competition.

The Dales were characterful then. Among the characters was Jackie Holme, a blacksmith living at Austwick who had attended t'smiddy at Horton for a quarter of a century. Jackie had developed swearing into a fine art and none of the swear words he used seemed unduly offensive. Once, in my early days, I was waiting for a bus at Clapham with Jackie (who then also had the local smithy) when Jack Swale, using a Council van, gave us a lift. It was in the middle of the monsoon period. Jack drove with the verve of Jehu, the Biblical charioteer, and when the van went through a flood, the displaced water cleaned the windscreen. At Austwick, Jackie left the car mutteringly. Instead of thanking Jack, he said: "Next time, Swale, go by t'bloody road."

Swearing was commonplace among quarrymen. One of them, nick-named Old Gen, collected a set of picture cards issued with Woodbine cigarettes. He posted them to Messrs Wills with a rough-and-ready note asking if there was a prize. The reply was – no, but what shall we do with the cards? Gen scrawled a note to them: "Send the buggers back."

From Jack Lambert I heard of the privations suffered by farm men. A man throwing hay backwards as he moved across the field was considered to do a better job than if he had used a hayfork, a practice that was common elsewhere. The farmer would not permit his men to carry lamps because he said they were uneconomical. Jack Airey, a local strongman, carried a nine-gallon barrel of beer (costing 9d) from the Crown Hotel to the farm where he was working, a distance of two miles. When a turf-barrow sank into the ground at peat-cutting time, and the wheel was broken, Jack picked it up and and carried it with the words: "If tha wean't be a barrow tha'll have to be a basket."

Inevitably, the dale had a ghost, more precisely two ghosts – a man and a white dog. They lived at Knight Stainforth Hall and, on moonlit nights, talked between the hall and Dog Hill. En route, they crossed the Ribble on Stainforth's celebrated packhorse bridge. A local toper, seeing the ghosts, is said to have remarked: "Behave yourself. Or I'll have another drink and send you away."

Bleak Midwinter

The most interesting Dalesfolk were those living at t'back o' beyond. Tucked away at the heads of little dales, out of sight of their neighbours and in some cases out of sight of the sun for several weeks in the year, were families adapted to solitude and privation. These social units, as they would now be called, were held together by the farmer's wife.

If snow arrived, there was nowt to stop it. Children sang: "Aly aly aster – snow, snow, faster." Old folk remembered when it was said: "They're plucking geese i' Scotland and sending t'feathers here." George Jackson, who had a cottage at Castle Bolton, in Wensleydale, woke up to find snow had drifted up to the height of the bedroom window-sill and noted: "The feeling was peculiar. A Pompeiian situation, emphasised by deathly quiet. I was nature's prisoner in my own house." The postbox at Beckermonds, in Langstrothdale, was covered with snow for six weeks. It had just been cleared before the blizzard raged.

In autumn, the old men consulted signs of what might be a bad winter. With a profusion of autumnal fruit like blackberries, and everywhere a sheen of scarlet from hips and haws, the Dales sages shook their heads and forecast a bleak time. "Owd nature's makkin' sure t'birds hes plenty to eat", they said. In winter, it wouldn't just be tewtlin' [putting down a few flakes] but stourin' [snowing with a strong wind behind it]. In Swaledale, where such terms were once used, people might be teeavin about [wading through snow]. The sloppy stuff that came with a thaw was known as "snaw broth".

Many of the lile farms, tucked away in folds of the fells, are no longer in use. If they have not been left to the wind, rain and frost, they serve other purposes. Such is the case with Cosh, in a world of its own, two and a-half miles beyond Foxup, which itself has a remote setting at the head of Littondale. Cosh has long been part of the huge farm of High Birkwith, in North Ribblesdale.

The seasons brought their special delights to Cosh – tewits and curlews in spring, black grouse into the meadows in late summer, the pageant of fading vegetation in autumn, the clean, healthful days of winter. If a blizzard raged, Cosh could be a wild spot. Halliwell Sutcliffe, the writer of romantic prose about the Dales, visited Cosh in the bleakness of a snowbound day. The barking of a farm dog indicated in that austere landscape that something was alive after all! "A sudden bend showed a hollow in the uplands and in it stood a stout farmstead. Children were playing in the snow. A buxom farm-wife ran to the door, to learn what the dog's warning meant. The contrast between the loneliness that has been and this present human warmth was bewildering."

Those children who were out at play had a round trip of six miles to school at Halton Gill, where in wet weather the teacher arranged for their clothes to be dried off by the stove and provided with toast at dinnertime. Two of the girls from Cosh, then the home of the Brown family, lodged at Halton Gill from Monday to Friday. When their brother was five, no lodging place was available. Mother kept him at home until he was seven.

Early this century, Cosh had a mere 18 acres of meadowland, also two cows and a horse. The income was derived from sheep – 500 hardy animals through the winter and an additional 700 belonging to other farmers that benefited from a change of pasture and the summer flush of grass in high places. Robert Campbell would take a horse and cart to Settle once a month to collect provisions. They cost no more than three gold sovereigns.

When the Campbells had gone, the Browns moved in. William Brown and his family thought nothing of walking five miles from Cosh to Horton-in-Ribblesdale to catch a train or of driving some of their Swaledale yows the ten miles to the market at Hawes. A month's supply of food was left at Foxup by T & A Stockdale of Hebden and collected by the Browns, using their own horse and cart.

A staple food was pork. When the pig they reared was to be slaughtered, John Cowan of Halton Gill was summoned. John insisted on having a lile drop o' whisky "or the pig wouldn't cure properly." Several days after the animal was killed, John and several farmers arrived to cut it up, after which they played cards - whist, sometimes nap - for the rest of the long winter night. Coal was carted, five hundredweights at a time, from Grassington railway station, a round trip of 24 miles. It is little wonder that the Browns of Cosh were keen to dig peat as fuel.

Robert, his son, told me a story of a protracted snowtime when 450 sheep were in danger of starving. William Brown gathered them up, mounted his pony and drove the sheep across the white landscape, seeking an area clear of snow where a farmer might provide him with

Bolton Priory, Wharfedale.

grazing for a copper or two a sheep. The first night was spent with friends at Neils Ing, "back o' Penyghent". The sheep were then driven into the Ribble Valley and grazing was found for them around Wigglesworth. In 1917, when snow and ice sealed the grazings at Cosh, one sheep spent three weeks under snow and lived to bleat the tale. That sheep, a ewe, died at the age of fourteen when she blundered into a dipping tub at a time when there was no one to rescue her.

William Brown gisted [summered on another's land] about 50 cattle belonging to other farmers. The most striking were cattle belonging to the Pratts at Hawes. William took his surplus ewes to Hawes market, 10 miles away. He was not averse to walking back with them if the trade was not to his satisfaction. The house cows were milked by hand, the milker sitting on a three-legged stool, with the bucket between his knees, cap with the neb at the back as he pressed his head against the warm flanks of the cow. In winter, he worked by candlelight.

My wife's mother was a Bushby from Kettlewell. They were related to the Bells, who have helped to fill many a Dales churchyard, including the biggest of them all at Aysgarth. In my *Dalesman* odyssey, I several times sat by the Wharfe as it negotiated one of its nursery stretches in Langstrothdale and pondered on the old farmstead of New Houses, where lived my wife's great grandmother, who was called, amusingly, Isabella Bell. She was as tough as they come, as indeed she had to be. A requirement of any Dales housewife was to bring up a family on next-to-nothing or, as one dalesman said, "on porridge and mouse-muck."

It was hardly as frugal as that in the home of the Bells, thanks largely to Isabella. She hit on a novel way of providing her family with pork products at virtually no charge. She rode a horse over Fleet Moss to Hawes, bought two piglets and reared them, largely on household scraps. When they were slaughtered, the meat of one pig was kept for family use and that of the other was taken to Hawes to be sold. The money received was used to buy two more piglets. And so on...

The Beresfords were among the most numerous of the Dales families. I was fortunate enough to know Frank, who latterly lived at

Hellifield. I used to camp him [spend a while in his company] and heard he was born in Langstrothdale in 1900 to George and Jane Beresford, who had just moved into the farm called Cowside House. George had a good horse, a cart and a sled that, made by Joe Raw of Kettlewell, could be horse-drawn with equal facility over spring grass or hard-packed snow.

Jane bore George lots of children. They were delivered by Mrs Roland Parker, of Deepdale, who had no formal qualifications as a midwife but was more relaiable than the Hawes doctor. He had to make the gruelling journey over Fleet Moss, the highest road in the Dales. With eight little Beresfords, the farmhouse at Cowside was always crowded, especially as George kept the provender for his cattle in the little parlour.

On to the fire went a few peats dug from Little Fell and coal brought from the pit on the moor near Threshfield, the coal being lifted straight from the mine shaft on to the waiting carts. In her busy round, Jane had no time to clean the black kettle which dangled from the arm of a reckon. When her family had dispersed, she decided to clean the kettle and was delighted to find it was made of gleaming copper.

Ben Lofthouse of Cray delivered the mail to the Langstrothdale farms. He kept the White Lion Inn and conveyed the letters by horse and trap. Ben was noted for keeping a good trotting horse. Any letters for Cowside were placed in a recess in the wall of a roadside croft. The postman then blew a whistle and, in case it had not been heard, placed a white stick upright on the wall so that the Beresfords could see it.

George Beresford died in April, 1905, aged 48. It was a time of privation for dalesfolk – a time for them to go into semi-hibernation until conditions improved. Wool was being sold for a miserable $2^1/2$ old pence a pound. George died quickly, without fuss, from appendicitis. His body was borne to Hubberholme, to lie among his kith and kin. Jane left the farm the same year. Cowside, a farmstead which had throbbed with life, is now uninhabited.

While playing an old tape-recording of a conversation with Annie Mason, of Gayle, I heard again her account of horse and trap journeys from Burtersett to Garsdale railway station. She drove her father, James Pratt, cattle dealer, to t'Junction so that he might entrain for Scotland, where he proposed to buy farm stock, mainly cattle. He was given a special meal when he turned up at the Caledonian Hotel in Lanark for the 60th successive year.

James had the respect of the farming community. When in partnership with T T Iveson, he started the auction mart at Hawes. It succeeded the old system of selling cattle and sheep in the main street. Sovereigns jingled in the dealer's pockets. A firm hand-clasp "sealed" a bargain. Annie also recalled for me when, in the back-end of the year, her father bought some Scottish sheep. Pure Scotlanders, he called them. After arriving by train and being driven to Hawes on the hoof they were turned out to graze Wether Fell. "We got overstocked with sheep in those days, and some of them were wintered at Brimham

Rocks, above Nidderdale. I remember one winter when there was a big snow as they were due to come back."

Other farmers' sheep were being wintered far from home and were due back home as snowflakes danced in the air. It would take several days to move the stock belonging to the Pratts. "When they had been two or three days coming," said Annie, "I was sent up to beyond Gayle on horseback with two bundles of hay, one on each side of the horse. I would use this hay to 'tice [entice] the sheep down. I also had some food – ham sandwiches and various things – for the men to eat. I took a thermos flask, which mother had bought in Liverpool. It was the first we had seen or known about. She made some coffee, put some rum in it and poured it into the thermos flask."

Annie soon made contact with the sheep and the Pratts and Fawcetts, who were in attendance. They were crossing Fleet Moss from Langstrothdale. Each sheep was treading in the footsteps of the one that had gone before. "I went up to Dick Fawcett and asked him if he would like a drop of coffee. He put the thermos to his lips and, of course, it was full of hot coffee. 'What the devil's in this?' he shouted."

"We had no trouble shedding off [separating] Mr Fawcett's sheep. When they came to his gate, they 'shed' themselves off. I got to the bottom of the hill and looked back. I could see a dark line of sheep all the way down the slope."

When I felt adventurous and my old Ford car was in reasonable order, I would drive into Teesdale, seeking the head of the valley, where spring gentians flowered near the cores of old snowdrifts and the reservoir that robbed this area of its wild beauty had not even been considered. It pleased me to know that half the upper valley belonged to Yorkshire, which – at Mickle Fell – stretched out a finger to tickle the ribs of Westmorland.

I parked the car at a trackside, among the tufty heather, and walked across bird-busy moorland, listening to the crowing of grouse and the melancholic whistling of golden plover. A small bridge crossed the head of Cauldron Snout, where the river went white with fury as it negotiated a staircase of whin sill. A little further and I rounded a corner to see Birkdale Farm, presiding over herb-rich meadows, which drew sweetness from limestone in an area consisting mainly of the fluty basalt. Brian and Mary Bainbridge were in their second tenure of this remote farm which, astonishingly, was in Westmorland.

To reach the parish church, the farmers of old had to follow a track to High Cup Nick and walk around the edge of this stupendous gorge to Dufton. A funeral party who did this, with granny's body borne by a fell pony, were annoyed when, at Dufton, as they warmed themselves up at the inn, the pony slipped its halter and wandered back to Birkdale. The keen-eyed grandchildren shouted joyfully: "Granny's coming back!"

Mary Bainbridge, who came into this area as a lass from Gateshead, paused while working in the garden at the back of the house. She then told me of Birkdale's curious geographical position. Until local government reorganisation in 1974, it was near the meeting place of three counties – Yorkshire, Westmorland and county Durham. There had been a time when Brian walked half-bred sheep to Appleby, by way of the rim of High Cup Nick. It is related that a shepherd boy directed his father to the imposing gill in these words: "Weel, gang ower t'moor, an' ye'll com ti a greeart goolf [gulf], an' it oppens out inter toother coontry."

During their first years at Birkdale, the Bainbridge family shopped in Middleton or Barnard Castle. The children who were attending school walked to Widdybank Gate, where a school car met them, They stayed at their granny's during the week, returning to Birkdale for the week-end or holiday time. The owner of Birkdale transformed a rutted track into a well-surfaced road in 1959. He hoped to re-set the slates of the farmhouse and excavate ground at the back of the house so that, for the first time for years, no floodwater would run through the house.

In 1962, the Bainbridges were building up the flock and started the winter with about 400 ewes. Snow fell and during the clear, sunny, bit-

Dales sheep at one of the autumnal sales.

terly cold days that followed three-quarters of the flock perished. That springtime, there was an unnatural quietness. Scarcely a sheep bleated. Much more recently, snow had fallen from a clear sky in April. Mary told me: "It was a lovely day on the Thursday but by Friday morning we got up to find it was snowing. By dinnertime, we couldn't see a thing."

The sheep, shocked by the impact of the storm, and still suffering from the after-effects of recent injections, decided to lamb all at one. "They were dropping lambs in the snow...We put them in the buildings and we had a house full of lambs. I was taking milk out of a ewe and feeding any lamb, just to keep it going. And all the time I was thinking: what if the ewes don't take to their lambs when conditions improve?" She need not have worried. When the ewes and lambs were turned out, they soon sorted themselves out.

The year before I joined the magazine, 1947, was to be etched into the mind of dalesfolk. The area experienced The Big Snow. The storm began in early February and was especially severe in the Yorkshire Dales. (I was serving in the Royal Navy by Cromarty Firth, in northeast Scotland, where there was but a sprinkling of snow and hard frosts).

G S Sweeting, who lived in Littondale, took a scientific interest in the weather and recorded that it was not until March 27, a period of almost eight weeks, before the snow-cutters cleared their last big drift. All over the Dales, men struggled to clear roads. Drifts up to six feet high were encountered in the dale, with over twice that height across moorland roads. When cleared, painstakingly, by human muscle and shovel, the cutters had the dispiriting sight next morning of the roads blocked once more by wind-blown snow. In places, it was possible for the snow-cutters to hang their coats on telegraph wires.

The effect on the hill sheep was devastating. Some farmers lost hundreds of sheep. Sheep which had been overblown, and yet had room to move and with an air-hole to the surface, fared better – if they were found in a reasonable time – than those which had remained on the surface and froze to the ground. A farmer saw a ewe struggle from a drift with a dead sheep frozen to its fleece.

Walden, an off-shoot of Wensleydale, has one end open to a north-easter and the other end to the moist prevailing wind, which comes from the south-west. In February, 1947, the farmer at Kentucky [the topmost farm] expected a delivery of coal. The merchant, noticing a few flakes of snow in the air, postponed the delivery until the following day. That night, a blizzard clogged the dale with snow. The Kentuckians were marooned for weeks. A large tree was felled to keep the home fires burning. They had a pig to eat and a horse to carry them on limited journeys.

I asked Edith Carr about its effects at Capon Hall, one of the big sheep farms on Malham Moor. Capna, as it is usually known, stands near the watershed at an elevation of over 1,000ft. Long before snow flurries arrived, Bob and Edith Carr's family had prepared for such an eventuality as though for a protracted siege, for "every winter you could reckon on a good snowfall, with the road blocked."

Snow lay on the ground when she had first visited Capna. It was November. "I went by horse and cart. Down in the valley, all was green, When I got to the top of the hill near Capna Barn, which was then a landmark, I couldn't believe what I saw. There was unbroken snow." Hence the urgency with which, in future years, they stocked up the farm for a winter siege. Five or ten tons of coal, in big blocks, were dumped so as to be handy to the kitchen. Bags of flour and oatmeal, plus tins of this and that, occupied every inch of shelf-space in the kitchen.

The Carr children, who attended school in Malhamdale, were not to know, in 1946, that when they broke up for the Christmas holidays they would not return to school until after the Easter holidays in 1947. The snow came in February, when snowdrops appear in Dales gardens but, on Malham Moor, the farmers reckon that winter was only half over. They anxiously checked the stock of animal fodder.

A cruel wind brought the snow, which stuck. "It was blowing and snowing. If the wind stopped for a short time, there came this terrible hard frost. All the sky was red." Teams of men who attempted to clear snow from the road had their efforts negated when, by night, the cruel wind blew in from the fields yet more snow. When a roadman had the misfortune to fall into the path of a snow-plough, and was killed, the body was carried into Capon Hall, where the parlour became a temporary mortuary.

The Carr family was employing a German who had been a prisoner of war. He set off with Tony the horse to collect some provisions from Langcliffe post office, in North Ribblesdale. The horse, but not the rider, had returned by nightfall. Frank Carr went looking for him. Collecting a storm lantern, he set off down the field. Cries for help were heard. The German was found struggling in deep snow. On the following day, his course through the snow was marked by discarded items of food. When, after weeks of privation, the Malham Moor families were desperate, the postman who walked from Settle every third day reported hearing on the wireless that the RAF were to drop some food and hay. "We had to make a big cross out of combustibles in the front meadow and when we heard an aeroplane coming we had to set the cross on fire. The postman said the airdrop would take place on the following afternoon at three o'clock. So we made this huge cross in the field and soaked it with paraffin and oil. We waited. At three o'clock, everything was quiet. An hour later, the 'zoom, zoom' of engines was heard and into view came Dakotas, based at Dishforth, with their loads of provisions for people and stock."

Quickly, Bob and Edith made the fire. The aircraft circled several times, flying quite low. Doors were opened and RAF personnel could be seen quite distinctly as they waved to the Malham Moorers. First came boxes, containing groceries, which split up on hitting the ground. "We didn't mind about that. It was food. We could pick it up later." There followed bales of hay. As the planes were still circling, the result was a huge circle of hay on the snow.

One day, Bob Carr went out of doors and returned quickly. "Come here," he said to Edith. She joined him. He said: "Just listen". The fluty call of a curlew cut through the still air above the snow.

Bob added: "T'curlews are coming back. We'll soon be all right."

The snow went quickly from low ground but ligged [lay] on Fountains Fell until the middle of June.

Dales Ways

Dalesfolk I met were not as solemn as they looked. Each had a daft story to relate. Many tales were imbued with fantasy. Jack Moore of Hawes mentioned to me Old Hebden, the watchmaker, whose top price for repairs was thruppence. He related that a man who went skating on Semerwater fell though the ice where it was unexpectedly thin. As he surfaced, he collided with the ice and cut off his head. A man standing nearby put it back in place and it froze into position. Later in the day, the skater was sitting in front of the fire at home when he blew his nose. His head fell off!

At Keasden, west of Clapham, I was told the fantastic tale of a local sheep-washing when, on the morning it was to take place, the farmers reported their dogs were missing. Dogs were needed to round up the sheep and retain them near the dub created when the beck was dammed. It was here that sheep were thrown in and, once soaked, had their wool ruffled by a man standing waist deep in water. This not only cleaned the wool but removed from the fleeces bits of grit which had been picked up on the moors.

With the dogs missing, the work could not proceed. However, the father of the man who told me the story suggested the dogs might have gone to the moor already, and so it was. "Aye – they'd rounded up t'sheep and driven 'em down to t'dub. One dog was in t'watter, weshin' t'sheep. Another dog was chuckin' 'em in. Somebody said to my dad: 'What was your dog doing?' He said: 'It were going round wi' t'bottle o' whisky'."

A district like Keasden retained its old-time flavour long after other areas had embraced more modern ways of farming. Around Hell Gill, where Yorkshire gave way to Westmorland within sight of Wild Boar Fell, the old ways prevailed. I loved to walk along the old highway between Cotterdale and Mallerstang and then seek out the farmstead of Cumpstone Hill. This "spot" was on a ledge overlooking the valley. T'owd farmer, a bachelor named Jossie Atkinson, reminded me what he had said many times before – that it was t'same elevation as t'Settle-Carlisle railway, which could be seen across the dale.

Jossie had a "pot" foot and the other leg was apt to get "gey tired". To spend a day with Jossie was to have t'auld days brought gloriously back to life. Most of our talking was done in his kitchen-cum-living room, where a huge fireplace incorporated an oven and wash-boiler, a flagged floor with pegged rug and a large table made of deal, which was scrubbable, though Jossie was not too particular in his housework. Two easy chairs had springs that twanged as we sat.

Jossie had occupied Cumpstone Hill for over half a century. His greatest adventure was when he served in the Army during the 1914-18 war. He once had a housekeeper but now lived alone. He retired from farming when he was 72 and was now 86. His special claim to fame was as a drystone waller. He enjoyed the work except when the weather was wet. He didn't like standing in a puddle. He remembered when hired shepherds kept their eyes on the flocks and when he used to trudge round the fells in hot weather, looking for maggoty sheep. Farmfolk were forever looking at their sheep. "They could nearly always find summat wrang."

He'd fetched peats from the moor in a coup-cart [a sled with wooden sides]. Peats were grand on baking day; they were terribly hot. "If there was a lile bit o' red in t'bottom of your fire and you broke a peat up, it started off practically right away." Jossie went to a hill-end pit in nearby Cotterdale for coal. "Bogeys ran in and out of t'mine. Each bogy held eight hundredweight, which was tipped into your horse-drawn cart. The charge for a cartload was 3s.6d. Cotterdale coal came in small bits. "You poured it on to a hot peat fire. When it had caked, you had a stab at it wi' t'poker."

Jossie's farmhouse had a beef-baulk [a space above the fire where salted meat was dried]. "They salted beef, same as bacon, and then they could eat it a long time after. There were no butchers round here then, you know. I butched a bit after leaving t'Army. A man in Grisedale had about a hundred wether hoggs [young male sheep] in November. "He butched six every Monday morning and took the meat to Hawes. I used to hing [hang] some hams in t'beef-baulk." Every family reared a pig, of a type that was larger and fatter than they are today.

Fat was worth more than t'bacon to t'auld folk. "I killed one here when t'last war was on and, using that oven, I rendered down twenty-eight pound o' fat. By gum, it come in useful did that; you see, we were rationed for lard and, being a big fat pig, when you fried you could get a potful oot o' t'frying pan. We made chips by peeling potatoes and cutting 'em in slices, about a quarter of an inch thick. We put pan on t'fire and a lump o' bacon fat in. Them chips were different altogether to what chips are now.

When Jossie told me about old-time remedies, he mentioned that if a cow calved but did not clean [get rid of the afterbirth] within five or six hours, he used to get a pint of cream and add a tablespoonful of salt petre, mixing it well. He administered the mixture from a cow horn, the one he used for dosing stock, and the "cleansing" was not long in coming. If the potion did not shift it, another dose must be given 12 hours later. "But it nearly always worked first time." Years later, I mentioned this to a farmer with a large herd who was worried about a cow that had not parted with the cleansing. The desperate man tried Jossie's remedy. And it worked!

Until the 1930s, the main recreation of many daleheaders was a trip to town on market day and an appearance at the local agricultural show. Most of them socialised at t'chapel, usually one of the Methodist variety – a plain little building, with a steep roof, as though to accommodate the exhaled breath in hymn-singing, and a porch stuck on as though it had been an afterthought. Dalesfolk liked their prayers to go straight to their God. As one of them said: "We don't believe in middle-men." The hymn-singing was accompanied by a lady sitting at a harmonium, usually of American manufacture. One organist produced strains which were unfamiliar to the local preacher who, in the homely way of Methodism, leaned over and said: "Nay, doesn't ta think tha can give us a more up-to-date tune?" She replied: "You can't have it more up-to-date than this. I'm makkin' it up as I go on."

The man who bestrode the fells during the week might be one of the local preachers, backbone of rural Methodism, who was thinking up a sermon. He would deliver it powerfully to people he knew. As an old lady said disparagingly of a parson with a string of degrees behind his name: "I'd rather have a chap 'at preaches than yan 'at teaches." The story is told of a Dales local preacher who was cycling into a headwind as he travelled to keep an appointment at a fell-end chapel. He prayed to God that the wind might change direction. It did. He had a headwind on the way home!

Kit Calvert, whose religious alliance was with the old Independency, being one of the "faithful few" at the Hawes Congregational Chapel. He recalled how, during the 1939-45 war, he had motored over Buttertubs Pass each Sunday throughout an inclement winter to take the service at Keld Chapel, which otherwise might have closed. On foggy nights he drove slowly, with the car window down and his head protruding from the car. He was not looking, for the headlights were dimmed to conform to wartime regulations, but was listening for the sound of the tyres on pebbles. If the sound stopped, he applied the brakes, knowing he had left the road.

He loved to lapse into Wensleydale dialect. He had translated part of the Bible into his native tongue. If anyone challenged this, he said he was following a good example. "Jesus spoke in dialect." So he would quote from his translation of St John's Gospel, Chapter 21, wherein Jesus "showed Hizsel yance maar ta t'disciples aside Tiberias Tarn." They were fishing. He called out: "Lads – hey ye caught owt?" They shouted back: "Nowt!" So he said: "Kest yer net ower t'reet side ev t'booat an' ye'll git a catch." They followed his advice. There were fish in plenty.

Kit was not short of a bob or two but, like many folk up t'Dales, he wasn't a show-off. I never saw him without a tie, though his clothes hung on him like old friends, which they were. He was no fashion-plate, with his gummy smile and grizzle-grey face, bright eyes and wiry hair which almost shouted out to be combed.

I first met this archetypal, clay pipe-smoking, dialect-speaking dalesman on t'bridge ower Gayle Beck at Hawes in Wensleydale, at a time when cars were still uncommon and there was plenty of time to get out of the way of the next vehicle. Kit took a while to coax a glow in the bowl of a new clay pipe, which he'd carefully packed with black twist. His little dog, sensing a long conversation, flopped and, in its fitful sleep, chased imaginary cats across the open spaces of its mind.

Kit was a character. He expressed his own distinctive personality at a time when Dales life had peacefulness and charm. Kit died in 1984 but is still well remembered if only as the saviour of the Wensleydale cheese industry in the 1930s. In 1953, when he built a new Creamery, the work cost him £15,000. The place was austere. When I called for a chat we could hardly hear each other speak as empty milk kits were dropped on to solid concrete. The voices of the staff echoed through unlagged rooms.

Kit's picture is prominently displayed at the modern Creamery in Hawes. The old way of making Wensleydale cheese, as recounted by Kit, was to take the milk warm from the cow directly to the cheese-kettle, transporting the milk in a back-can. "An aunt of mine put a few pints of scalding water into the kettle to lift the temperature to 85 degrees. Then she put in rennet [the starter]. Cheese was made only from the milk taken from the cows in the morning. The afternoon milk was for making butter."

We sometimes discussed the type of cheese known as whangby, which was so chewy [tough] it had to be attacked with an axe. Whangby cheese was made of either blue [skimmed] milk or half of skimmed milk and half composed of new milk. Kit said: "A greedy person put up the night's milk for butter. He took the cream off that milk and put the skim milk into the morning's milk for cheese-making. So the cheese didn't get the right percentage of butterfat. It was hard and fit for nowt but cooking – or to be given to the farm man!"

Kit also had his famous little bookshop, overlooking the main street. His passion for books had begun when, at the age of nine, he howled at his father, who was a struggling quarryman, and demanded – of all things – a Collins clear-type dictionary, price one shilling. Father bought the book. In later life, Kit was a great frequenter of sales. He showed me a prized tome and remarked: "I had to buy over six hundredweight of books to get this...I didn't bother to bring the others away." When we first met, in the early 1950s, Kit had soon switched the conversation to books.

Two antiquarian booksellers had helped him collect the works of Matthew Willis, a local poet. They were published under the title of *Mountain Minstrel*. The volume was found and purchased for 10s. Within three months, Kit saw the local dustman going to the tip with a barrow-load of books. "I offered him a shilling to tip them out and re-load after I had looked through them. He found another copy of the rare book of the poems of Matthew Willis.

Kit was a generous man who frequently gave books to friends. He presented a magnificent collection of Yorkshire books (total value nearly £3,000) to Yorebridge Grammar School – and then joyfully set about making another collection. The selection of foisty books in his shop at Hawes was excruciating, being in the main either dull religious works or Victorian romances, their pages yellow and brittle because the paper used for printing had been of poor quality. All the best stuff was in Kit's personal collection.

An American appeared in the shop, looked casually along the shelves, then leapt with joy as he drew out an old book which, it seemed, he had sought for years, all over England. He asked Kit how much he wanted for the book. Kit said: "Sixpence". Incredulous, the American said: "Surely you could charge much more than that?" Kit replied: "Appen. But I'm not having anyone going back to America saying he'd been diddled [cheated] at Hawes."

When there was no one in the bookshop, a purchaser was invited to leave the money in a chapel collection plate. Or his old friend John Mason was on duty. John, an ex-railwayman, who clattered about in clogs and had taught himself Greek, referred to the bookshop as Hawes University, of which he was the bursar. I was at Kit's house one day when John brought along the day's takings – sixpence.

Kit's Bookshop, which still exists by name in premises down a near-by ginnel, and has a rather better class of book, was a notable cal 'oil [gossiping place] on Tuesday, which was market day at Hawes.

Daleswomen have not received much publicity down the years, but this has not applied to Hannah Hawkswell, of Baldersdale, who was featured in an official report about the Pennines as a hill farmer who was living on less than £200 a year. Her spartan life was written up for *The Yorkshire Post* by Alec Donaldson and much later appeared in a Yorkshire Television documentary called *Too Long a Winter*. Hannah than had a minor part but her worth to television was soon recognised, leading to series of programmes, including Continental and American travels.

My first meeting with Hannah Hauxwell was memorable. She was late to bed and late to rise, spending much of her day with her few cows. Hannah was living by herself in the family farm, which had become terribly run-down. She craved for sunshine during the short, invariably cloudy summers and the long, dark winters. As she remarked: "In summer I live. In winter, I exist." It became a custom for me, when on holiday, to send Hannah a picture postcard of a scene with an azure sky.

On successive visits to the Hauxwell farm in upper Baldersdale, I followed a winding track between rush-bobs, under the unblinking gaze of horned sheep, and in due course arrived at Low Birk Hatt, which now stood near a huge reservoir, known to Hannah as "my Mississippi." A knock on the door brought the sound of yapping from a terrier-type dog. Hannah was heard rebuking it for its bad manners.

She was then in her early sixties, prematurely grey but with the rosy complexion of someone who had regularly doused her face in beck-water, stimulating capillary action. If the beck in the field at the back of her house ceased to flow, as was the case in summer, she resorted to the reservoir. Television pictures had prepared me for a scrow [untidy appearance] in her living room. There had been little time to spare for housework. Said Hannah, with a grin: "I think I was born in a pickle."

As the years went by, Hannah began to travel, each trip leading up to a television documentary and eventually to a whole series of documentaries. She was taken to a garden party at Buckingham Palace, where she saw the Queen, though at a distance, and had "brown bread and butter, a lovely little pancake, a cheese scone, a piece of fruit cake and some chocolate cake. Being me, I had TWO cups of tea."

Hannah had no romantic ideas about life on a Dales farm in the old days. Of a haytime of the 1930s, she said: "It was a tough, sloggy time. We were always understaffed. One bad haytime, we 'packed in' on November 17. Then we hadn't got it all." Even on Christmas Day, which she invariably spent by herself, without a trace of self-pity, she was absorbed by "beast-work". She would say: "I wish it was always summer."

When she left the farm for a pleasant house at Cotherstone, I asked her about her daily routine. She hadn't got one! Hannah confessed to being no better at getting out of bed than she had been at Low Birk Hatt. She smiled, then added: "Me and time do not go well together." She enjoys trips off, such as on signing sessions connected with new books about her life and experiences. Queues of record length developed at the selected bookshops and also at Malham Show, where she was once the chief guest. Hannah did not hurry. She ordered her life by the old Dales dictum that "if a job's worth doing – it's worth doing well."

For some years, she insisted, when book-signing, of making a thorough job, complete with greetings and the date. At Skipton, when it was time for the bookshop to close, the queue was so long that it was kept open and coffee was served to those waiting patiently on the pavement outside for their autographed books.

In the 1950s, I occasionally saw an exceptionally tall, tweed-clad man walking down the High Street in Skipton. He was Sir William Milner (1893-1960) who, standing 6ft 7in high, was head and shoulders above the crowd of shoppers. This somewhat shy bachelor, who had been a familiar figure in the Craven Dales since the 1920s, was usually dressed in well-worn tweeds, overlaid by an old mac. See him at close quarters, and his unkempt appearance hinted at the lack of a wifely influence. Yet by bearing, William Milner was an aristocrat, being the 8th Baronet of Nun Appleton. His godmother, Queen Mary, frequented the antique shops of Harrogate.

As a handsome young man, living in London, William Milner enjoyed visiting the Dales. His favourite valley was Wharfedale. Pedalling a heavy bicycle, made especially for him, he would stay at the George Inn at Hubberholme. He practised as an architect with a professional partner, who had the unforgettable name of Romilly Craze.

In due course, William confirmed his love of the Dales by transforming what had been a rambling farmstead on a south-facing hillside near Skyreholme into stately Parcevall Hall, where he might live the life of a country gentleman. As a Christian with a reflective frame of mind, he created a chapel that was just large enough for a priest, for Sir William and for Bracken, the much-loved Labrador. In the chapel he placed a statue of Our Lady of Walsingham.

Parcevall Hall stands at 1,000ft above sea level in an area with a probing wind. When he first saw the old farmstead, it was neglected. On the hillside were some sheepfolds. The fellside was scattered with wheezy thorn trees. Structural work, including the addition of two wings, was undertaken during a period of industrial depression. The costs were relatively low.

A sub-contractor, Mr Cross of Shipley, provided a team of workers from the Keighley area. Dales craftsmen were also recruited. Masons were specialists and labourers did the pick-and-shovel work, transporting material by horse and cart. In the end, the work cost about £40,000. The rooms of the hall were decked with fine furniture, much of it bought from Frank Laycock, a Skipton antique dealer.

The Hall, with its view of moorland capped by Simon's Seat, is offset by a range of gardens. In front of the house is a formal garden – and a glorious view of Simon's Seat, crowning the moorland ridge beyond a little valley. Beside the house were wilder places that in spring were to be bright with daffodils. An enthusiastic gardener, Sir William was a friend of Reginald Farrer, the "father" of rock gardening. He had the best possible advice on rock plants and rhododendrons.

When Parcevall Hall was leased to Bradford Diocese as a retreat, I enjoyed my visits and chats with local people who remembered William Milner as an imaginative as well as a practical man. For example, when he was to plant daffodil bulbs, he gathered around him everyone who might help, including an upholsterer who arrived at the hall to cover some chairs. William then filled a large sack with bulbs, tied the mouth loosely and walked through the orchard, swinging the sack round his head. The bulbs flew out. Wherever they landed, they had to be sunk in the ground. An exception was those that lodged in the trees.

Living by the Pen

Harry Scott wrote the monthly *Dalesman's Diary*. He reviewed the books, kept the accounts and left the rest to me - until he decided we must have another drive to get advertisements. An early advert, in full colour, had novelty value. The printer left a quarter-page gap that was filled by fixing to it an adhesive advert, not unlike a large stamp.

Harry bestrode a financial tightrope and despite his training as an accountant he was not emotionally suited to being a businessman. If one of the bills he sent out was not paid, he was known to quietly drop the matter. One year, *The Dalesman* would make a small profit and next year there was a small loss. Envelopes were re-cycled. Ribbons for the typewriter were used until they were in tatters and carbon paper until, after much pounding in a typewriter, it resembled lace curtaining.

Reader interest was keen. Harry liked to think of every reader as a member of a big happy family. Though the circulation was climbing steeply so, alas, was the cost of printing and distribution. I could understand why, as the printer came to discuss the percentage increase for the following year, the normally affable Harry became tense and his clenched knuckles whitened.

Having decided to boost income with more advertisements, we would work feverishly at it for an hour or so until the mood passed and Dorothy Scott appeared with cups of coffee and consoling words. Our circulation was not lightly won. Each morning, I typed out a hundred names and addresses from the telephone book so we could send out specimen copies of the magazine to the folk whom Harry presumed were the wealthier members of the community. There were mundane tasks like keeping up-to-date the cuttings files which Harry had begun in his freelance days during the 1930s. A neighbour who borrowed a hacked-about copy of *The Yorkshire Post* described it as "the filleted edition".

Going to the post office was a pleasant task when the sun shone and villagers were in the mood for a gossip. I raised my cap to the local dipper as it stood on its favourite beck-washed boulder and curtseyed. From the numerous trees and shrubs came avian whistlings and twitterings. Curlews chased the cumulous clouds across the blue vault of the sky.

Grannie Cross would be emptying a furled umbrella of its cuttings and roots collected from other gardens. Her problem was finding space in her garden for those that had taken her fancy. The gardens of Clapham were of the cottage variety and even the crumbling walls were floriferous. Not for some years would the fashion for window boxes and hanging baskets give the place, and other villages in the Dales, the Cotswolds look. Mrs Vant had a pet duckling she had hatched out in her cistern cupboard. It waddled after her to the limits of its strength and was then given a ride in her basket.

Ben Hudson clambered on to a wall-top to mount a horse. He would give an anguished cry if the horse moved and the gap between it and the wall widened. The cry was also heard when, having started milking, there was a power cut and a clatter as the elements of the milking equipment he had painstaking attached to cow teats fell to the ground. Ben and Jack Winton had an uneasy relationship. It was a matter of territory. Ben kept footloose hens. Jack had a garden in which he nursed young plants for the grounds of Ingleborough Hall. Ben said hens had a right to roam. Jack said he had a right to put down poison for the slugs. The hens were persuaded by a new wire fence to stay at home.

I fitted into my weekly routine two of Harry's freelance jobs. They brought him perhaps five guineas a week. One was a hangover from the *Herald* days. For years, I wrote the newspaper's leading article. In days when editorial comment in papers and magazines tends to be shrill and political, it is pleasant to think of a time when we were concerned with drystone walls, with litter, with the terrifying increase of a farm labourer's wage to £3 a week. How on earth could the hard-pressed farmers absorb such a wage?

I had also to supply half a dozen gossip notes under the heading of *Craven Man's Diary*. These were trivialities bound together by cliches. The "old Craven man" was still on hand to give a topical introduction to ancient themes, for Harry had further stocks of yellowing newspaper cuttings from his early years in journalism. Each week, I ended with a brief amusing tale plucked from the *Dalesman* archives, such as that about two men who were walking in the Dales when one of them fell down a pothole. His anxious friend shouted down to him: "Have you broken anything?" Came the reply: "There's nowt down here to break."

The second regular item was an article for the Saturday edition of the *Yorkshire Evening News* of Leeds, a newspaper long defunct. Under the heading "In my Yorkshire Valley", subtitled "From the Little House", it consisted of everyday tales of non-existent dalesfolk living in an imaginery dale. It was based originally on Clapdale, taking in the village of Clapham and the valley leading up towards Ingleborough.

Having control of life in a fictitious valley was fun. It was a Dales version of the radio programme *The Archers*. A character called Old Nathaniel hobbled into the feature about once a month to roundly condemned modern life, which wasn't a patch on what it was like when he was a lad. There was to be an off-shoot of Old Nathaniel in the cartoon figure, Old Amos, who became a *Dalesman* celebrity, brought to life through the penmanship of Rowland Lindup. Each month, Amos would utter words of wisdom, such as "Ah reckon that women like to be flattered. Men likes to flatter thersens." When he was in philosophical mood, he might remark: "Ah reckon that folk who think t'least, talk t'most."

Each instalment of the *Yorkshire Evening News* feature was illustrated by Godfrey Wilson, an elderly artist who used Indian ink on coarse paper, pasting down a drawing on to heavy-duty cardboard which was un-fileable. Godfrey lived at Stainforth, in North Ribblesdale. In his young days, he had been a keen climber and potholer. The rooms

Pack Horse Bridge, Thorns Gill, Ribblehead.

of his house were named after underground systems in Yorkshire. He cycled over from Stainforth on an ancient bike. We provided him with a cup of coffee and waited patiently for him to muster the back of an old envelope and stub-end of pencil, then offered ideas. Godfrey, who hated to be rushed, would repeatedly say: "Wait a minute".

He was paid a pittance for impressions of Dales life which had been formed in the 1930s and continued unchanged for at least three decades. His Dales farmers had not been beguiled by changes in fashion. They continued to wear jackets, fustian trousers, leggings and boots. They had broad-brimmed felt caps and, without exception, were pipe-smokers. The only time one of Godfrey's farmers took the pipe from his mouth would be when he wanted to eat or sleep.

At a time when money was tight, filling the magazine cheaply was a key to its survival. It was here that a loyal band of readers helped with informative letters. An early letter had mentioned an association between Bramwell Booth, founder of the Salvation Army, and the fisherfolk of Whitby. Our correspondent claimed that Booth had originally wanted to call his religious denomination the Salvation Navy. Each reader had the feeling of being a member of a big family. There were critical letters, an early one referring to a doleful piece headed: "It always rains in the Dales". The author promptly submitted an equally amusing successor headed "It never rains in the Dales."

Arthur Raistrick, a premier Dales historian, submitted authoritative articles about this and that – and was paid for none of them. As a Quaker, he had a conscientious objection to helping the war effort, as he might do should he have to pay income tax. He and his wife, Elizabeth, had resigned themselves to a wartime of High Thinking and Simple Living.

Harry's recipe for a good issue was one which had a good solid article, such as one sent in by Arthur, two articles of much shorter length and lots of "fillers" and readers' letters, the last named being presented under the homely title of Readers' Club. The tale-enders – bits at the ends of pages – had been inspired by those in the then much-respected

Readers' Digest.

A stream of articles arrived. Most of them must be returned, invariably with a personal letter. Harry was several times tempted to use what he called the Chinese form of rejection: "Your honourable contribution is too good for our pages." Book manuscripts were sometimes retained for further consideration. The successful author was he or she who persisted with inquiries. One manuscript that had been the subject of a wearying correspondence was eventually sent to the printer unsubbed. It was a disaster, not because of its literary content but because Harry, anxious to get it off his desk, fixed a retail price that turned out to be slightly less than the cost of production.

When we moved from Fellside to a converted range of estate workshops we had bought cheaply from Ingleborough Estate, Dorothy Scott regained her lounge. In the new premises, I saw less of Harry. No longer was there a brief early morning chat in the dining room as Harry and Dorothy sorted through the morning's post amid pots of marmalade, pats of butter and pieces of toast. Harry had acquired an inner sanctum, with an approach passage giving early warning of visitors. He just had time, before the visitor arrived, to slip into a bottom drawer of his desk the ancient periodical he had been perusing.

He enjoyed talking to friends and visitors. In old-time Leeds, he and Dorothy had joyfully attended performances of plays by J B Priestley. The gruff Bradfordian who had left the city for fame and fortune had an affable welcome for the magazine which appeared in Volume 1, Number 1. It was ironical that when JB Priestley visited *The Dalesman*, it was as *my* guest. In those days I was living in Settle and commuted over Buckhaw Brow, a delightful experience on sunny days when, going north, I had a prospect of the blue hills of Lakeland and, returning south, surveyed the grand limestone sweep of Giggleswick Scar. For a time I went home for lunch, which was a welcome break in the day's routine. On a spring day in 1965, I returned home to find Freda, my wife, flustered.

She had been baking. Her hands were still dusty with flour. Two small children, home from school, were at their noisy best. She intercepted me at the front door and whispered: "J B Priestley and Jacquetta Hawkes are in the front room." And so they were. The famous Yorkshire wordsmith was sucking the stem of a pipe. Jacquetta was quiet and serene. Mercifully, JB was not incinerating tobacco or smoke would have poured out from the bowl of his pipe like that from a West Riding mill chimney when there was a rush-order for cloth.

A friend of ours who had commissioned the piece mentioned my interest in the Dales and JB and his wife called for a chat. They wandered off for a meal, anxious not to disturb our domestic routine at such a crucial time. I discovered that the café they visited was gloriously old-fashioned, pure *Good Companions*, down to the menu, propped against a sauce bottle, featuring such items as "Plumbs and Custard". Jacquetta decided she wished to visit Victoria Cave. I drove one of the literary celebrities of England over Buckhaw Brow in my old car and left him with Harry Scott. When I returned, half an hour later, I discovered that both men had been smoking and could scarcely see across the office.

JB knew the Dales of old. He had visited the region as a boy with his family. He returned to his native West Riding after the trauma of service in France in the 1914-18 war and persuaded the Editor of *The Yorkshire Observer* to let him write a series of articles based on a walking tour. He was paid "a guinea a time". JB joyfully walked "out of the iron and blood and misery of war into wonderland, still magically illuminated by memories of my boyhood."

On a later visit, Dick Chapman of Bainbridge taught him how to catch crayfish. Dick was a man JB loved to meet. He said of him: "Dick belongs to my generation and has all its fiery energy and optimism." JB once stayed with Marie Hartley and Joan Ingilby, who had written extensively about the Dales. The two ladies had just invested in a television set. One evening, their visitor asked if he could switch it on. Naturally they agreed. He watched a boxing match – and gave Marie and Joan a round-by-round commentary.

Janet's Foss, Malhamdale.

William Riley (1866-1961), who contributed to the magazine, had, like Priestley, some strong Bradford connections but unlike Priestley had immense charm and strong religious convictions. He was *too* sweet for my taste. William Riley was famous when, as a small boy, visiting Grannie at Bradley near Skipton, I was drawn into a packed congregation at the Methodist chapel on Anniversary Sunday to hear him preach. His name was boldly presented on a poster. Passers-by could not help but notice it: William Riley, followed – as surely as night followeth day – by the words "Author of *Windyridge*". So many people turned up to hear him that extra seats were needed, some being placed in the pulpit alongside him.

In the world of William Riley, the sun always shone and everyone was nice to each other. *Windyridge*, which appeared in the autumn of 1912, was a literary double – a first book that became a best-seller. He wrote it to console two bereaved sisters, reading it in parts, as he wrote it. The story was of a London girl visitingYorkshire, the location being inspired by Hawksworth, "on the far side of Baildon Moor." It was the first book to be published by Herbert Jenkins and more than repaid the publisher's faith in it. Jenkins believed, when he accepted it, that the W Riley, on the title page, was a woman. Riley was fond of telling a story against himself – of the visitor to Hawksworth who entered a cottage where "Teas" were advertised and asked the old lady who served him if she had read the book. She replied: "Aye, and I think nowt on't. It's nowt but a pack o' lies from beginning to end."

As a young man, Riley explored the Craven district. In a *Dalesman* article he wrote: "I wanted to see, with my own eyes, the caves and chasms, the potholes and ravines, the bogs and swamps, the glens and moorlands, the streams and waterfalls, that other explorers had seen and had described so vividly in their books." At Ribblehead, he watched the Scots express cross the viaduct and at Grassington he met Barber Bowes, who was said by one disgruntled visitor to cut hair with a knife and fork.

Charles John Cutcliffe Hyne, the novelist creator of an entertaining little seafarer called Captain Kettle, spent his later years at Kettlewell in Wharfedale where, periodically, I chatted with his daughter Nancy about his life and literary achievements. (When I last saw her, in 1998, it was her 96th birthday). Cutcliffe Hyne contributed a piece to the first issue of *The Yorkshire Dalesman*. This prolific writer was born in Gloucestershire but reared in Bradford, spending much of his adult life in travel, from the Arctic and Lapland to the Congo and the Spanish Main.

He had introduced Captain Kettle into a story called *Honour of Thieves*, which was serialised in *Answers*, a lively magazine founded by Alfred Harmsworth. The seafarer, who was surely named with Kettlewell in mind, had an insignificant part, but when the last of the articles appeared, Harmsworth told the author "that little red-haired sailor man was the best touch in your story." Cutcliffe Hyne was immediately offered a Captain Kettle series, at "thirty bob a thousand [words]" but this offer was tartly refused. His Lordship said he never paid authors more because it only drove them to drink. Eventually, Captain Kettle appeared in *Pearson's Magazine*, at 50 guineas each.

Cutcliffe Hyne wrote the tales over a spell of 40 years and Ward, Lock published them in book form, selling over five million copies. This represented only part of his output. He was heard to say: "I write my stories anywhere. I have written them in the Atlas Mountains and leaning against a lamp post in Bradford."

I was working at the *Craven Herald* at the time of the writer's death in 1944 and had to attend the funeral, taking a bus from Skipton to Grassington and then walking to Kettlewell, arriving stiff-legged and weary. Old folk in Kettlewell recalled when, in the 1930s, he panned for gold, as he had done in the New World. He found some gold but in such small quantities they hardly repaid his efforts. He suggested that the clear becks of the Dales should be used to develop a water cress industry. His scheme for railway camping coaches was eventually taken up, but Morecambe Bay still awaits the application of his vast scheme of land reclamation.

Lying east of the A65, between Ingleton and Cowan Bridge, was what I tended to think of as Conan Doyle Country. It provided material for various articles, the most important being that of the Doyle, the creator of Sherlock Holmes, our best-known sleuth. Masongill, a village tucked away at the end of a narrow, hedge-flanked road, is a bonny place. The road, a cul de sac, continues beyond the hamlet to the start of a turbary [peat] road, not very far from where a group of wind-harrassed trees marks out Marble Steps, a pothole undoubtedly known to young Doyle.

At Masongill, for some 30 years, lived Mary Doyle, the novelist's beloved mother. She moved to Masongill with her young family in 1883 and was friendly – some say, very friendly – with the squire, Dr Bryan Charles Waller (1853-1932) who lived at Masongill House. Mrs Doyle had strong literary connections. Her brother-in-law, Richard Doyle, had designed the cover of *Punch*. Waller had had a magnificent library containing several thousand volumes, including Robert Southey's *The Doctor* which, published anonymously, dealt in part with the Ingleton district. For a time it was believed the author was Waller himself.

Conan Doyle wrote frequently to his mother. One estimate puts the number of letters he penned to her as 1,500. He was married at the local church, Thornton-in-Lonsdale, a building that is unusual in having a mini-spire on the castellated tower. Doyle's bride on August 6, 1885, was Louisa Hawkins. Details of the marriage are on view in the porch of the church. Doyle introduced Sherlock Holmes to the public in *A Study in Scarlet*, published in 1887. Interestingly, two clergymen in the Masongill area at the time were the Rev T Sherlock, of Ingleton and Pastor Sherlock of Bentham.

Local gossips linked Mary Doyle with Dr Waller to the extent of believing that Conan Doyle was his son, which is improbable. He visited Masongill from time to time. Mary, pert and pretty, would doubtless sigh when he got on to the tiresome topic of Dales fairies. She left the hamlet in about 1920 and died, aged 83, at the home of her famous son, whose death occurred in 1930.

Waller breathed his last on November 14, 1932. He had left instructions that his body should be conveyed to Thornton Church in his much-loved dog-cart, but this was found to be unsafe. The bier was used. Tenants helped to fill the grave. Before this was done, one of them was reported to have looked at the coffin of the martinet which reposed there, and whispered to a friend: "Now then, there'll be no 'yes, sir' and 'no, sir' where you've gone."

A former servant girl who was at Masongill House at the time of Waller's death said his widow instructed that papers and diaries belonging to the squire should be burnt. A bonfire blazed for hours as accounts of his deepest thoughts were incinerated. Perhaps among that mass of paper was the solution to some of the local mysteries.

That servant girl had good reason to remember Thornton-in-Lonsdale church. On a February night in 1933, a blizzard was raging. She had been out with her young man. They hurried in the wintry weather for she must be back at Masongill House by 10 pm. They kissed and parted. He set off for his home at Ingleton and saw Thornton Church burning like a torch. Which is why, should you go there, you will find a feeling of newness about the place. The fairies have deserted it.

Marie Hartley and Joan Ingilby, who have painstakingly researched Dales life and industry, were the authors in 1951 of *The Old Hand-Knitters of the Dales*. Knitting had been an important domestic industry. Theirs was a true collaboration. They wrote a chapter each; then exchanged the chapters for criticism and revision. Marie told me: "I am best at the broad sweep of a book. Joan is a stickler for detail. We accept each other's criticism in the right spirit and work in perfect harmony."

Rather more than 60 years ago, Ella Pontefract and Marie Hartley, of Wetherby, had formed a writer and artist partnership, rented a disused farmhouse at Angram and gathered material for a book about Swaledale. The two young women lived opposite each other at

Wetherby; and shared accommodation during studies in London. When, over sixty years ago, they rented a farmhouse to research their Swaledale book, there was not a drop of rain for the whole month. Returning to the valley for a shorter period in October, they completed their work on what is now a classic study of a Yorkshire dale.

Ella wrote in her diary that they were staying at "a funny rambling old house with all the windows facing the wrong way." Marie recalls: "When we wanted a bath we were loaned a tin one, on the understanding that it was returned every Saturday so that Tom, our landlady's youngest child, might have his weekly bath." The book, published by Dent in 1934, was written by Ella, who had recently studied folklore at University College, London, and was illustrated by Marie.

In 1935, they followed up their *Swaledale* success with *Wensleydale*, living in a caravan they parked at Bainbridge. The caravan, which they named The Green Plover, had first been based at Shaw Paddock, near the source of the Ure and not far from the busy Settle-Carlisle railway. Each evening, as the two women went to their beds, a regular steam-hauled express thundered by.

In 1938, they bought Coleshouse, a cottage at Askrigg, and adapted it to their needs. A third book, *Wharfedale*, was published. Ella died in 1946 at the age of 48. Two years later, Joan Ingilby – herself a poet and writer – joined Marie at her Dales home. The nucleus of the Dales Museum at Hawes, which atttracts thousands of visitors each year, is a collection of Dales byegones assembled by Marie and Joan.

I have had some pleasant moments at Coleshouse, which stands by the hill road leading from Askrigg into Swaledale. An unpretentious cottage, built of local materials, it was fittingly adapted to be the home of creative folk. The wrought-iron gate shut with a clunk, not a clatter. In spring, the garden was spangled with celandines. Marie and Joan had been "genuine gardeners", though a Dales village at an elevation of 800ft above sea level is not the best place for the cultivation of flowers and vegetables. Their first garden was in a cal-garth, a name possibly derived from calf. It was extended. "We used to have vegetables –

our peas were marvellous – but we got beyond doing it so we're all roses now."

One of Marie's earliest Dales experiences was climbing Buckden Pike in June 1927 to observe the total eclipse of the sun. In the late 1920s, "four of us, good friends, had a walking tour, as was the fashion. In the party were Ella Pontefract, Olive Bedford (Marie's cousin), Eva Johnson and Marie. "We started from Richmond with rucksack on our backs and wore good strong shoes, not boots. We stayed the night at Reeth, then went up to Keld where they stayed with the Waggetts and the Rukins.

Said Marie: "The charge was 6s a night, including an evening meal. It was lovely food. I do remember cakey-puddings – fruit base with a cakey top. From here, we crossed the Buttertubs Pass and went down to Hawes. We used to think that Hawes was the farthest place you could get. It was just nothing but farmers. Thence it was over the tops to Wharfedale. At Kilnsey, we took a taxi down to Skipton railway station." The rucksacks carried by Marie and her friends held the minimum – "you know, a pair of bedroom slippers."

Marie, on the last occasion I met her, reflected for a moment about Wensleydale, then said: "There are wild roses up the roadside, as they were when we first knew the dale. The roses are still lovely."

Linton-in-Craven was the home of two contrasting Dales writers – Halliwell Sutcliffe and Arthur Raistrick. Fortunately they did not live here at the same time. Sutcliffe, author of a very popular, romantic book, *The Striding Dales*, was indeed a Striding Dalesman, ever active. In his literary work, he did not let a few facts get in the way of a good tale. Arthur was pedantic and, invariably, accurate. From his high position as a Dales authority on geology, archaeology and history, he was prone to be highly critical of others.

I doubt whether Halliwell Sutcliffe made a fortune out of his writing, though in a literary career which began in 1893 and ended with his death in 1932, he saw into print an estimated five million words, including about 30 novels with Yorkshire moorland settings. In his lifetime, he was much respected by local people. The few survivors of that age recalled for me a man clad in a Norfolk jacket and breeches who was either walking or cycling.

He spent his daytime amassing ideas when cycling along the narrow roads of Wharfedale or working in his large rock garden. After dinner, around 8-30 pm, he would slip into his study and stay there, writing, for most of the night. He teased from his mind the ideas and experiences of the day. Guy Ragland Phillips, a Yorkshire journalist whose family knew the Sutcliffes, told me of seeing him at his Linton home. "He was lean and wiry from the constant physical activity in which he delighted. And to my eyes, even when he sat in a folding garden chair on the terrace, he seemed to be very long."

His writing carried the reader along in a good mood, as with his description of the river Wharfe, which "rises in the high lands round about Oughtershaw, and runs between steep hills that widen out with each mile passed. They call the stream Brown Wharfe, because the rains come often, washing down the red-brown peat into its waters..." Burnsall Church was packed for his funeral service, but do not look for his grave in the local churchyard. When Halliwell Sutcliffe died in 1932, his ashes were scattered on the moors where (as he had written) "the lean lands rake the sky."

Arthur Raistrick, a good friend of *The Dalesman* from the earliest days, was born in Saltaire in 1896. His great grandfather, Charles, had been a well-known cattle dealer – and a skilful poacher. He was one of the men who had introduced the small Irish cattle into the area, collecting them after they had been landed at Liverpool. Arthur was taken to the Dales as a baby. He could remember his Dales experiences from the age of six.

The earliest Raistrick letter in my archives is a copy of one written to *The Yorkshire Dalesman* magazine in 1940. He mentioned that for the duration of the war he had given up his Readership at University College, Newcastle-on-Tyne. He and his wife would be experimenting with simple living. He might even buy a cycle for increased mobility.

Arthur subsequently used public transport where possible. He travelled by car as a last resort.

Home Croft, where he and Elizabeth had many happy years, was a converted barn at Linton-in-Craven. A wide view took in the heights of Greenhow and Fancarl Crag, round past Elbolton and other reef knolls to the line of Thorpe Fell. When the barn was purchased for conversion into a house, it was found to be almost devoid of right angles. Elizabeth and Arthur settled down in their beloved Wharfedale with an Aga cooker, a boiler for radiators "and as much electrical equipment as we could afford – vacuum cleaner, washer and refrigerator." It was an impressive list considering they had been purchased early in the war.

I was never likely to catch Arthur in bed in the morning. He rose early, spending the first hour listening to classical music played on his old gramophone. Then he settled down, in a 10ft square study, which was so crowded there was no space for a door to swing. Instead, a double curtain cut off the study from the hall. The public-facing side of their barn-cum-house was little more than a blank wall with a door set in it.

Arthur was forever sending me critical letters. Whenever I knocked on the door I braced myself, having already decided what I would say and do if he proved difficult. The door would open to reveal a serene man who smilingly invited me into the house. Several times my visit coincided with baking day. Elizabeth, herself no mean writer and historian, chatted with me in the kitchen after providing me with coffee and well-buttered scones. Elizabeth had a fund of good Yorkshire stories and told me of a funeral procession that was passing up Skipton High Street. A well-dressed and somewhat arrogant lady visitor pushed her way through to the front and inquired in a superior voice: "Who is dead?" A nearby dalesman replied: "Him in't box, missis."

Arthur was faddy [finicky] in the matter of food. Elizabeth was forever saying that he didn't like this or that. When she had but recently died, I was on a visit to my favourite fish and chip restaurant in Skipton when I found Arthur tucking in to deep-fried haddock and chips. When Arthur was living alone, he and the house began to look careworn. Some of the Wharfedale ladies who had attended his various classes on local history, and became known as "the gang", got into the habit of visiting him on Tuesdays for talk and tea.

When I called during the Elizabethless days, Arthur would invite me into the main living room (formerly the mewstead of the barn) to inspect documents and illustrations connected with his latest research. One day, I saw every level surface was covered with old lead-mining photographs that he was assembling for an important picture book on the industry.

I never came away from a chat with Arthur Raistrick without having been stimulated in some research I was doing and which I had mentioned to him. He did not always provide answers but suggested courses of action. Once we discussed the name Wild Boar Fell. I thought it sounded too romantic to be used by the Norse folk. He mentioned the difficulty the first Ordnance Survey party would have in filling in placenames on the map. It was a case of Southerners trying to understand the speech of the Westmerians.

Another day, I mentioned *Deep Harmony*, a favourite West Riding hymn tune. As a lad, Arthur had met Handel Parker, the composer. Some of Arthur's uncles were members of the hymn-writer's male voice choir. He was invited along to a rehearsal on the evening that, according to one of his uncles, "Mr Parker's trying out a new hymn tune on us." It was almost certainly *Deep Harmony*.

In his later days, Arthur, with his fine grey hair blowing in the wind, resembled an Old Testament prophet. Someone described him as being like a piece of his own rugged mountain limestone. When Arthur was 90, I contacted some of his close friends, including "the gang", and published messages from them as a birthday tribute. Helen Lefevre, a neighbour at Linton, remembered him as a gardener. "Each day he would be running up and down the steps outside my cottage to the plot of ground in the almshouse garden which he rented. He would be digging or bringing back flowers and vegetables. He had of course been hard at work at his own study and research from about 4 am until breakfast-time. In his house garden he had a rockery on which he and his wife had some of Reginald Farrer's plants. His cherry trees are at this moment a riot of colour."

Arthur warmly acknowledged the tributes paid to him. I was pleased to note that "I have long counted you among my close friends." He signed the letter "Arthur". This notable historian and anti-quary, author of 39 books and over 150 pamphlets, died in 1991 at the age of 94.

Sir Rupert Hart-Davis, who for 35 years was a much respected London publisher, first set eyes on the Dales in 1947 when his old friend and colleague, the writer David Garnett, lent him his cottage at Butt's Intake on Whitaside, from which there were splendid views of Swaledale. When I visited him at the Old Rectory at Marske, near Richmond, he told me: "David thought that Swaledale was the most beautiful place he had ever seen; so did I, the moment I got there." This was after an eight-hour journey from London on indifferent roads. At the time of my visit he was 78 years old. He passed the quiet days in contentment. "I always wanted to live in a beautiful place and read and write books. Now I am doing it. In my old age, my dream has come true."

Just after a war in which he saw military service, the holidays in

Swaledale were a tonic for mind and body. The war had little effect on Dales life. The only complaints he heard in the late 1940s was of a shortage of cigarettes. "Rationing was still officially in force, but the local grocer always gave us a little extra butter and sugar. We were incomers and strangers but he was extremely good to us."

Eventually, the Hart-Davis's rented a holiday cottage at Thwaite. Then they discovered a ruined cottage high on Kisdon, overlooking Keld. "It had one room up, one room down, and a short of hutch off it. It had been empty for 50 years. There were about eighteen inches of sheep-droppings upstairs and downstairs...I managed to buy it, after a tremendous tussle with Willie Whitehead, who lived at Pry House. The main snag was that two fields went with it and I didn't want the two fields." The cottage, put in order, was used for holidays from 1955 until 1964, when they moved to Marske, recognising that a cottage at the top of the hill was no place for a person to spend old age. It could not be reached except with a Land Rover. "Otherwise, you had to walk up, which took twenty minutes with rests and rather less time walking down."

Hart-Davis had subscribed to *The Dalesman* for a great many years. When I visited the Old Rectory at Marske it was without an appointment. I apologised. He smiled and said: "If you had written for an appointment, you wouldn't have got it." I had my interview – plus coffee and biscuits – in a room holding his library of 16,000 books. Hart-Davis's account of the acquisition of the 23-room former Rectory amused me. He was driving to Richmond on the top road one day when he saw the house, which still belonged to the church. It had been empty for six years. "I went to the post office and inquired about it. They let me have the key. My wife and I went over it and thought it was marvellous, though in a terrible state. Cows had got in downstairs and it was full of dead birds, prayer books, soot and things. Dirty. Horrible."

The house and front field were coming up for auction at the King's Head in Richmond. "I came up from London for the auction. Only one man bid against me. I got it for £4,200 and felt that if that man had not been there I would have got it for £2,200 because no one else was bidding. The field at the back was purchased from the Church authority.

Before it could be sold, they said he would have to get a faculty to de-consecrate the path from the gate to the new churchyard. "I wrote back and said there is no path and there never has been a path; it's a green field. They then wrote back and said I needed another faculty to enable me to step over this path. I signed an enormous document. One clause said that no chickens would be allowed to run in this field. So I said to them: 'I've no intention of running chickens, but why not?'

'Oh,' was the reply, 'they might fly into the churchyard and dig up the graves.' Can you imagine such a circumstance? It took me six months to get them to sell it."

I have already mentioned my encounter with Thomas Armstrong, novelist. When I first saw him he was working in his garden. As with Rupert Hart-Davis, I had no appointment, but he cheerfully agreed to chat. His work in the garden had elements of civil engineering, for he had decided to pave with stone a garden that was now knee-deep in weeds. I was taken into the big Georgian house where he and his wife had lived for six of the 12 years they had had spent in the dale.

Until recently, Tom – the name by which he was known to his wife and family – had done all his writing in a small cottage in the court-yard. Now he had turned his dressing room into a study and he often worked there into the small hours. "The people in the valley always know when Tom is working," said his wife. "The light in his window is the only light for miles around! No, I don't go to bed and leave him to it. I stay up to keep him supplied with cups of tea."

The novelist reached for his pipe, kindled it, beamed at the opportu-nity for a short break from work and said of his writing: "It is hard slogging work. When I come to the end of a novel I'm physically and mentally weary. When I finished the 440,000 words of *King Cotton*, I was actually ill for two days." He found beginning a novel the most difficult part of writing. "Once I've got the first 3,000-4,000 words pinned down, I can steam ahead. On a good day I write about 10,000 words, working through the night." He did not like working in the afternoon. His friends could not understand how a novelist could for-get characters he had written about so fully, "but that's how it is with me. Once a book is finished and published, I'm done with it. I never read a book over again. I'm too busy writing another one."

One of the truly exciting moments at the *Dalesman* office in Clapham was when Harry Firth, our printer, arrived from Kendal with a small packet. He opened it up to reveal a well-illustrated book which had been entirely hand-written and hand-drawn. It was the first of what were to become the celebrated Wainwright guides to the Lake District. Wainwright insisted that the book should be printed exactly as he had left it, with not a line of type. He allowed me to print selected pages from this and successive books in our magazines. They benefited from the publicity.

Wainwright, the authorartist, who during the working day was in charge of the finances of Kendal Corporation, was a shy man. In the early days of authorship, he shunned personal publicity. Though best-known for his Lakeland guides, he loved the Yorkshire Dales and included them in three of the guides which followed the basic set. These were for the Pennine Way, the Coast to Coast walk he had devised and for a guide to the limestone country. He had by then become the proverbial legend in his own lifetime. He was quirky, crotchety, taciturn – and lovable.

He preferred to walk alone, in the spirit of Matthew Arnold, who wrote of "the cheerful silence of the fells". If Wainwright saw an approaching party of schoolchildren or ramblers, he tried to avoid them or slipped behind a boulder. In contrast with the modern rambler, wearing fashionable multi-coloured, all-weather garb, AW donned ordinary clothes, including a cloth cap and a well-worn raincoat with pockets large enough to hold his pipe and tobacco pouch. His boots were ordinary boots, with nails for extra grip. He used public transport extensively, never carried a compass and not only made the Ordnance Survey the basis of his maps but periodically wrote to them suggesting modifications. Some years later, if I used a map, however sketchy and though it was marked "not to scale" I got a letter from the Ordnance Survey reminding me of copyright and seeking a fee.

On our first meeting, which was by appointment, he had agreed to an interview. It never took place. He looked affable, whenever he emerged from clouds of pipe-smoke, but he adroitly dodged my questions. Half an hour later, I concluded that he did not want to be interviewed. Not for many years did he overcome his natural shyness and reserve and become a media personality. We met, now and again, or he typed me a brief letter, signing it (in green ink) first A Wainwright and then simply AW, a mark of friendship.

When, in 1988, I was about to retire as Editor of both *Dalesman* and *Cumbria*, Betty Wainwright brought him along to the *Dalesman* office for a chat. As she left to go for a walk, he said slowly: "I'll be all right. I think we'll find something to talk about." Perversely, I swung the topic from fell-walking to animal welfare. By this time, most of AW's thoughts about walking and the fell-country were well-known and I was familiar with his humour. Each year, I intended to find some bilberries and fresh sheep droppings to photograph them side by side. He had written that anyone who takes up fell-walking should be able to tell the difference between them. Bilberries taste the sweetest!

What we did not know for many years was that Wainwright had been in the Dales as early as 1938 when, still living at Blackburn, he travelled to Settle and trudged northward on the Pennines to Hadrian's Wall. He wrote up his experiences as *A Pennine Journey*, which was to be published (its text virtually unchanged) almost 50 years later. There were typical Wainwrightian forms of expression. In North Ribblesdale "my shadow was my sole companion". The church at Horton was "somewhat shabby" and reared its old head above the cottage roofs, "signifying that it has lost none of its pride." At Hubberholme, in Upper Wharfedale, he stayed overnight in the home of Mrs Falshaw, who had first scrutinised him as though he were "a visitor from another planet."

AW died in January, 1991. His last upland walk was on a day when it rained incessantly and he was wet and dispirited. He wrote: "The mountains wept for me."

Hill Farmers

On the marginal lands, once so neat and tidy, stand deserted farmsteads – mostly ruined, their roofs partly gone and timbers showing like the ribs of a sheep when the crows have had their fill. Crumbling drystone walls remind me of the old frontier between rough pastures and the moor. Some farmsteads are now in forest glades, the trees being neat rows of sitka spruce, which grows almost with the speed of rhubarb under grey Pennine skies. I had the eerie sensation, after pushing my way through an unbrashed spruce plantation, of finding a farmstead lagged with moss and ferns. The sight made me unutterably sad.

The farm had been part of the "fellside culture", where a host of Dales families faced up to thin soils, a high rainfall and long, long winters with a stoicism we can scarcely understand in these affluent times. It was a life which made no permanent demands on the land, was self-reliant and rich in close family relationships. Kick a man – and half the men in the dale would be nursing their shins!

Such a hill farm might remain viable for years despite its small area of inland and limited farmstock. A dozen cows - gentle Shorthorns, renowned both for beef and the quality of their milk – provided milk to be separated, the cream used for butter-making, for sale and barter, and the "blue" milk fed to the young stock – or, on larger farms, to the hired man. On the moor were tough horned sheep. A farmer knew his sheep as individuals, by facial markings and general appearance. When a visitor was amazed at this facility, the farmer said: "Nay – I reckon thou could pick out thy wife from a hundred other women."

Moorland peat, cut and stacked to dry, then moved to the farms by horse and sled, provided the bulk of winter fuel. Occasionally, a load of coal would be bought and painstakingly transported to the farm by horse and two-wheeled cart. In some cases, that five hundredweight of coal, used on special occasions, would last for years.

These uplanders, clumping about their farm wearing clogs, which were ideal for turning mud and "snow broth", were hard-working, God-fearing and with a community sense based largely on t'chapel. Dozens of little chapels served the updale areas where the influence of the Established Church was limited. I preached in many of them and remember the robust singing from old farmers who resembled Old Testament prophets. Their prayers were heartfelt, with muttered "Amens" to acknowledge any well-made points and, on one occasion, lots of "No, Lords" when the young preacher was proving to be too radical for the local taste.

When the horse died at a small farm, a neighbour took a collection from families living round about and a new horse was provided. They prized their stock to the extent that at some places, such as Cam Houses, near the headwaters of the Wharfe, the Lambert brothers were known to keep t'best tups in t'parlour. Cam Houses, once a distinct community, a collection of small farms on a gale-blasted hillside, now has only one occupied farm. A barn has been converted to accommodate overnighters on the Pennine Way.

Kit Calvert, the sage of Hawes, told me lots of tales about the place, which he visited periodically when his main income was derived from farming. Kit bought a white cow from the farmer and when driving it back to Hawes he lost it – in a blizzard. He had to return the following day to look for it.

Bob Lambert, usually referred to as Bob o' Cams, regularly went to Hawes market.

One day, thirsty but without money, he approached a man who was selling Model T Fords and showed interest. There was one condition – he would buy one if it could be delivered to the door of his home. The dealer assured him this could be done and provided Bob with the ale for which he had craved. When the car was to be delivered to Cam Houses, it foundered in soft ground long before it reached the farm-

house.

On one of my visits to Cam, I was introduced to a novelty, a radio-telephone, finely tuned to a transmission aerial just over the fell in North Ribblesdale. When the telephone crackled during a conversation, the farmer would say: "It's nobbut an owd sheep walkin' on t'skyline." Returning to Cam Houses after a long interval, I heard that when fire broke out in the "camping barn", and 999 was telephoned, the request for the fire service was answered by a station somewhere in Lancashire.

I enjoyed watching a Dales farmer hand-milking cows. The job seemed half as old as time. He had a three-legged stool and just before sitting on it he turned the neb of his cap to the back. As he milked into a pail, he pressed his head against the flank of the cow after attempting to curtail the swishing of the cow's tail. For such a tail was usually adorned with little pieces of dry dung which he called "muck buttons", which could sting if drawn across the farmer's face.

The last hand-milking I saw was at the Bordley Farm, the home of Tommy Birtwhistle and his family. I had been taking an afternoon service at a Methodist chapel near Burnsall. There was no invitation to tea, which was unusual. Having to take another service at Threshfield, where Tommy and his family worshipped, I drove to his remote farm. After tea, Tommy announced that it was milking time. I followed him into the shippon, expecting the machine-milking of a dozen or so cows.

This was a big sheep farm, with just two "house cows" on the staff. They were milked by hand and as he coaxed milk from the teats, I heard the rhythmic swish of milk against the sides of the pail. When we asked a well-known artist to provide us with a series of pictures of Dales farming for a calendar, it was published before anyone noticed that a man who was milking had no pail.

Tommy's cattle were Shorthorns. Another special memory of this breed was in 1986 when I visited Marjorie Longstaff at Deer Park Farm, Harkerside, high above the River Swale. She made cheese in the old way, the milk being from her two cows, Tiny, an eight-year-old red

Shorthorn, and Blackie, a matronly female. My arrival at Mrs Longstaff's farm was itself memorable, for I stepped out of the car into – silence. Then grouse began to talk to each other on the sunlit moor. Silence again. I was offered a sliver of Swaledale cheese and allowed it to linger in my mouth so I could enjoy its mellow, Shorthorny taste – the true taste of Dales cheese.

Darnbrook, a hill farm of 2,854 acres, now owned by the National Trust, was regarded as "back o'beyond" by many. It stood beside the road which snakes across Malham Moor and, just beyond Darnbrook, climbs a brant [steep] hillside, offering one or two sharp bends to test the traveller's driving skill. No other farmstead could be seen from the farmhouse, a building with mullion windows and a substantial porch.

Darnbrook was part of the historic Malham Tarn estate, owned by Lord Ribblesdale, of whom it was said he could ride from Gisburne Park, his mansion in the Ribble Valley, to Malham Tarn, without straying off his own land. When it was owned by Walter Morrison, he was in a party of people who explored a cave lying under the kitchen. We know this because when that cave was re-discovered, Morrison's name was among those inscribed on the walls. At Darnbrook, a motorist encounters a gate. Once there were 16 gates which, when closed, helped to separate the stock in the big upland pastures. In Victorian times the Settle doctor, who used a horse and trap, employed a coachman. Going to Darnbrook was a two-man operation.

The Robinsons farmed Darnbrook for many years, Henry, his wife May and five children flitted to the farm from Bordley in 1941. They were one of several Malham Moor families whose activities were regularly noted in *The Dalesman*. A year after their arrival at Darnbrook, the snow-dogs were howling and for three weeks the sheep did not see grass and had to be foddered with hay.

In 1947, when the weather was at its grimmest; when wind blew dry snow off the fields and piled it up on the roads and when the ground was "hard as iron", to quote a familiar Christmas hymn, an RAF aircraft dropped bales of hay. One of the Robinson "lads" told me: "You can't beat the place for bad weather, either in winter or summer." We discussed haytime. I heard there were 65 acres of meadowland. Was it enough to fill the barns? "It was enough for us to get in bad weather."

Jim Metcalfe, a native of Malham, had memories of byegone haytimes when virtually every job was done by hand. (Jim died in 1997, doubtless with many of his Dales recollections untold). He mentioned that porridge featured at virtually every breakfast and, at Darnbrook, porridge was served twice a day – for breakfast and as the first course for a hot evening meal. Everyone engaged in farming had his own scythe, "blacksmith laid", being adjusted to the size and style of the owner.

One of Jim's first jobs as a lad in Malhamdale had been to take a biscuit tin to the shores of the big tarn on Fountains Fell and collect some silver sand for scythe-sharpening. He would begin the return journey with a full tin and gradually whittle down the amount of sand as he wearied of the weight. The remaining sand was issued to Irishmen, who used long-poled scythes and sharpened them with a strickle – a square piece of wood that had been pitted with holes and was rubbed with greasy bacon. The scythesman then took some of the fine, hard sand from a bag and, spreading it on the palm of his hand, patted it with the strickle. The sand worked its way into the tiny holes and was held there by the bacon fat, forming an abrasive surface.

A Darnbrook haytime came when summer was waning. The yows and lambs had been kept in the meadows until well into the springtime and, as Jim said, you can't have it all ways, can you? As the oldest of the Robinson lads said: "We're always terribly late wi' haytime. We've eaten t'grass too hard and we've been late with the mowing." It was a time when men from the west of Ireland arrived in the Dales and hired themselves out for a month at a time at a fixed sum, the farmer providing board and lodging. If the weather was inclement, they did odd jobs, such as thistle-stubbing and bug-blinding [white-washing].

One memorably wet haytime, Henry Robinson, snr., anticipating a busy spell, travelled to Skipton and engaged two Irishmen to help out.

When they arrived at Darnbrook, they saw a weeping willow in the garden. One of them remarked: "It's a bleak spot. Trees are growing downhill". The War-Ag., set up to help promote food production, had been given the task of mowing the grass. They had "knocked over 40 acres down. And look at t'weather..."

Jim, who was asked to help, couldn't see any hay. He was told that when he got into t'field, he'd find plenty. "The stuff had been lying so long, fresh grass was growing through the old swathes. The only way to separate the two was to strike twice at each spot with a hand-rake." They began at the wallside and had not been long at work when Mary Robinson appeared at the field gate and announced it was dinner-time. It was decided they would work their way back to the farmhouse, going "t'longest way round" till they reached the gate.

It took them an hour and a-half. Jim recalled that the hay they pulled out was "as red as a fox – no good." It was none the less taken to the barn. "It wasn't worth much but up at Darnbrook it'd keep summat alive." Happily, the biggest half of the crop consisted of good hay, so "it made up for t'disappointment of t'first lot."

At New House, a farmstead tucked out of sight of Malhamdale and approached (patiently and with care) along narrow roads and a stretch of unmetalled track, Walter Umpleby tended his 65 acres in the old ways. His meadows, unsullied by artificial fertilising, dazzled the eyes with the tonal range of up to 80 species of wild flower. What I remember of the inside of New House was its neat and tidy old-fashionedness. Chatting with Walter in his living kitchen, I heard that breakfast, served on a well-scrubbed deal table, consisted, Dales style, of oatmeal porridge, home-reared bacon and eggs from free range hens.

Walter's wife, who had died some years before, made a pegged rug every other winter. Fragments of fabric from old clothes were attached, with the deft use of a wooden "pricker", to hessian stretched on a frame. Rug-making, a tedious job, did provide "a nice pastime...there was no television then."

Dominating the kitchen was a huge range, typical of an old farmhouse. The "firespot" was flanked by a hot water boiler and oven. Walter said Shuttleworths of Skipton transported the range to New House on a horse-drawn cart. The fire consumed five tons of coal per annum, being delivered to the farm "about August time", plus a bit of wood from a neighbour down at Gordale. Water transferred from the boiler to a bucket by "ladin can" was mixed with calf food. The farmer and his wife also "got washed from it" on bath-night, water being transferred to a hip bath.

Edith Carr regaled me with tales of Capon Hall – known locally as Capna – one of the lonely old farms on Malham Moor that, in the hey-day of cattle droving, was sometimes called Traders' Hill. Then, said Edith, "the wiry Scottish drovers passed with their lean, lank, long-horned cattle, mangy and scraggy after their weeks of walking from the Borders and beyond, through the long miles of the Pennines. They were heading for the Great Close, a 600-acre plot beyond Malham Tarn, where large sales of Scottish stock were held."

I first became aware of Edith's astonishing memory and poetic inter-ests when she appeared with me in a Granada television programme. By this time, her husband had died, her family was scattered, and she lived in a small house at Langcliffe. Subsequently, when I had a cam-corder, I recorded a year in her life as it applied to looking after sheep, from winter feeding and selling the wool "clip" until, in t'back end, she sold the sheep to a dealer. The deal was struck after the usual protract-ed Dales haggling. They haggled twice; once to fix a price and once for the benefit of my camera.

The bleached skull of a Swaledale tup was a gruesome feature of Edith's roadside garden and evoked the story of a walk across the "tops" with her daughter Anne. It was an evening walk. The skull was found among tangled vegetation near the path. Edith noticed the horn burn (RC) was still legible and realised with amazement that this was an animal that had belonged to her husband, Robert Carr, when they lived at Capon Hall, some 40 years before. Robert had been upset because this fine animal had vanished in the blizzard of 1947. The night she saw the skull, she thought about the circumstances and, rising from her bed at 5 am, she walked through miles, collected it, called it Rambo and mounted it on the outer wall of the house.

The Dales reek of sheep. Some of the best of the Swaledale tups were to be seen on parade at the sheep show held on Tan Hill in the spring. In the autumn, I enjoyed the atmosphere of the tup sales, at Kirkby Stephen or Hawes. They were held just before tupping time. The old-time farmers reckoned that a ewe mated on November 5 would drop her lamb on April 1. An early start is recorded where a Swaledale is being crossed with a Blue-faced Leicester to produce a "mule". But on the highest farms, where pure-bred 'uns are the rule, the tups are "loosed" about the 20th. The lambs are born when, hopefully, the worst of the winter is over.

Sheep farming on the broad acres of the Pennines is possible because, in the collie dog, the artful dodger of the skyline, the farmer has a rapid means of gathering the stock from thousands of acres of upland country. The dog is controlled by a series of cool, clear whistles – a sort of canine morse code – to which it reacts instantly. The sheep get to know the whistles and the working of the doggy mind. Not every dog has the aptitude for farm work. A farmer whose new dog was stretching his patience was asked: "Is your dog no better?" He replied: "No better? I reckon it's ten times no better!"

Another fretful collie-owner who was training his dog with little success finally gave up and shouted: "Come back. I'll go missen." Such wayward animals are exceptional. Mark Hayton, of Moor Side, Ilkley, used to say: "Let your dog think and be your servant – not your slave." Farmers tend to be a bit cagey about money, but I gather that nowadays the best dogs are valued at well over £1,000.

The strangest story I heard about a sheepdog was from the lips of Sam Dyson, a stalwart of the Yorkshire Sheepdog Society. Sam was for years a judge at the trials, when man and dog put their wits against a trio of sheep, driving them round various obstacles and finally penning them. Sam watched one man "put his dog off" to collect three big, heavy sheep, bringing them through the first obstacle. One sheep startled everyone by lying down and not getting up again. The trialist ignored it and continued with the drive. At the hurdle, another sheep fell to the ground and lay there, unflinchingly.

Sam considered there was no point in continuing to judge the trialist, but the man continued and made a valiant effort to pen the remaining sheep. The stewards found two sheep dead. As Sam said to me: "I bet there's no other man in England has done owt like that, is there?"

Exchanging a pair of low shoes for green wellies, I joined farmers and dealers at Hawes for the annual Tup Sale, at which 920 animals – young, handsome and virile – passed through the show ring in two days. Many of them would soon be on Active Service at farms across the North, for as I have mentioned, November is tupping time at the updale farms. "A change o' tup freshens t'breed," said a Wharfedale man. He was referring to the Swaledale breed, of course, which is a type set by selective breeding at the farms on and around Tan Hill.

Hawes, on the two days of the tup sales, became one gigantic parking lot for Land Rovers, trailers, cars and vans. I asked a grizzle-grey farmer if he was selling or buying. "I'se just watching," he said. Nearly everbody was talking about a recent sale at Kirkby Stephen at which one breeder took along 16 animals, which averaged £2,800. If I'd bought a tup with that sort of money, I'd be scared every time the animal sneeezed. I commented to the grizzle-grey farmer that there surely could not be that much difference between an animal which had just been sold at £1,200, an average price, and the next tup on view, for which bids petered out at £80. A smile flickered across his face. He replied: "Them 'at's bidding 'appen knows summat we don't."

Before the start of business, judging of the tups took place. There was a smile on the face of Tom Metcalfe, of Usher Gap, Muker, who had brought along what turned out to be the champion tup, a shearling, a year and a-half old. A steady procession of farmers called to view what was prosaically known as Tup No 403 in Pen No 33. It was, in truth, a superb animal, and would provide quality stock to populate the steep breast of land opposite near Buttertubs Pass. A Craven farmer told me how he had prepared his tup for sale. He dipped it, then used a powder to colour up the fleece, after which he carefully washed the face. Finally, he'd got "a rag wi' some meths on" to "clean t'white up".

Nowadays, farmers with valuable tups keep them under cover during the run-up to tupping time, anxious that two animals will not "git to fighting". An old dodge was to fasten a short piece of chain from one of the horns of an animal to a horn of another, so that scope for movement was restricted. Antagonistic tups face each other, then meet head to head with a thump that carries far on the still autumn air. A Craven farmer said: "I reckon if owt knows the miseries of a headache, it's a tup that's just been in a feight [fight]."

At the Hawes tup sale I attended, the bellman went on his rounds to announce the start of business. A last minute rush of tweed-clad bodies filled all the available space around the sale ring. The only man with space in which to move was the auctioneer on his rostrum. He sipped some thermos tea, tapped the microphone and began to intone. The first click, indicating the mike was alive, had stilled the babble of voices.

Clearly, this auctioneer felt he had to give the vendor plenty of time to display his stock or he would cop it [be taken to task]. A tup in the sale ring had nowhere to go but in circles, urged round and round by the owner so the potential buyers could study form. The first animal I watched had bright eyes, well-set legs and "a good square carcass". Contrasting with the black face was the white of the muzzle, with a dash of white above each eye. Massive horns stood out from its head like the handlebars on a bike.

In this game, much of the bidding takes place surreptitiously. A nod is as good as a wink. One man raised the price of a tup by £100 with a movement of his catalogue. "Everybody has a different way of bidding for the tups," I was told by Raymond Lund, one of the auctioneers who – born and bred in the upper Dales – knows a good Swardle when he sees one. There was no vocal dawdling. The bidding climbed in hundreds. "Six hundred, 700, 700 bid…" and so on to "2,100 away…"

A Sedbergh farmer had "come to git another tup" to augment the efforts of the resident animal for his flock, which was of only moderate size. He would be content with yan of t'cheaper 'uns as long as it was bright-eyed, well-marked, with a "squary" carcass and well-set legs that were good enough to'od up in a blizzard. At the pens, farmers assessed with well-tuned eyes and busy hands the quality of the tups on offer. A man stumbled and rested his hand briefly on the tup's back to steady himself. Or so it would seem. Yet during the second or two his hand rested on the animal's back, he had assessed the tup's body size, its weight and condition, also the density and quality of the wool.

During my Dales-wanderings, I saw the transition from horse to tractor. A Northern Irishman called Harry Ferguson introduced a tractor that was small, elegant, versatile and had "hodding back power", to quote a farmer I met in Walden, a tributary valley of Wensleydale who was referring to its low gearing. This made it safe on the fellside, where it effectively succeeded the Dales pony as maid-of-all-work.

It was not the first tractor I recall working in the Dales. We were invaded, during the 1939-45 war, by Fordsons, big powerful machines with rear wheels spiked so as to maintain their grip on the old pastures which, at government decree, were being turned brown side up [ploughed]. I have heard farmers speak about "t'lile grey Fergie" with such feeling they might be talking about a member of the family. The name of the firm became Massey-Ferguson, and now and again, even today, I see the red tractor produced at this time, but affection is reserved for the older type – the trusty Grey Fergie. It is to be seen on many farms, either working or parked in a corner of the yard, fringed with rust, as if the farmer could not bear to part with it.

The Grey Fergie was a handy little thing, though the footbrake was apt to slip when moist, such as with the coming of the dew to a hay-field. Then along came the All Terrain Vehicle – ATV for short, but known as a "quad" to most Dales farmers. It was initially a trike, with balloon tyres that gripped well and didn't hurt the ground. Now, with four wheels, a farmer can do jobs much quicker than he did in pre-motor days, when he would set off shepherding on foot and was away from home for most of the day. On his "quad" he roars up hillsides and along ridges at a fast pace. He is home in good time for lunch.

A farmer who passed me at speed, with a light alloy crook nesting beside him and his dog riding pillion, entered a field without the effort of opening the gate. He simply drove through a handy gap in the wall. The quad lurched and swayed a little as it was driven down a slope to a beck, which it forded with ease. The dog leapt to the ground and was soon on an outrun during which about 30 sheep were gathered. The farmer drove up the hillside to meet them.

A dalesman said one snag with a quad is its handiness. "I had one pinched. Aye. A walker passed through, then came back and chatted with me about my quad. Later that day, it had gone. And it wasn't insured." He had a newish machine in the farmyard. His face wrinkled with a smile as he said: "It wean't be so bad if somebody taks yon bike. T'insurance'll git me another!"

Dales farming altered radically with the accent on Big Bag Silage, the plastic bags, large and black, looking from a distance like giant slugs. The driver of an excursion coach tells his urban passengers, when passing a farm where big black bags are stacked in a corner of a field: "We're just passing a black pudding factory."

Artistic Endeavours

An invitation to address the Sedbergh Arts Society on its 25th birthday offered me a chance to do some mental stock-taking. I spoke about Dales artists whose work I know well. Most of them had escaped to the Dales from the towns. They were intoxicated by the landscape but frustrated by the transient weather patterns.

Professional artists made a living, but "nobbut just". A Dales farmer preferred oils to water-colours, for the simple reason that with the former he was getting more paint for his money. My old friend Guy Ragland Phillips took up painting – as well he might, being a grandson of Atkinson Grimshaw. Completing a commissioned portrait of the daughter of a Wensleydale farmer, he soon experienced the lament of an old-time artist that "every time I paint a portrait, I lose a friend." The father of the girl looked at Guy's impression of her, commended him on its quality – "by gum, it's grand" – and then asked: "Who is it?" Guy, picture under one arm, sneaked away.

We reproduced in colour J B Priestley's study of Ingleborough as seen from beside the Hawes road. Priestley, who was staying with Marie Hartley and Joan Ingilby in Wensleydale at the time, portrayed the flat-topped hill in its blue-grey mood. JB had taken up painting in the mid-1950s. He had a preference for gouache, which enabled him to use washes and also particularise.

He told me: "I love the broad open landscape of the Dales...But you do need a bit of sunlight to bring out the colours. I only paint on holiday. I get very cross when I can't do it." He looked peevish that day. I inquired about his most recent work and he remarked: "I've only done one sketch since I came this time, which makes me angry."

Those were unpolished, somewhat gruff, off-the-cuff remarks. Later, sitting before his trusty old typewriter, his fingers moved briskly, pipe

NORTH
YORKSHIRE

WOODLAND
DETAIL

smoke clouded the air and the ideas flowed smoothly. In an article about the Dales which was printed in an American magazine he wrote: "Let these tops, these slopes, these valleys, be seen through swift changes of sunlight and cloud, from thin mists to the angriest purples and blacks, and you have a scene, forever shifting, that entrances any sensitive eye and drives any landscape painter, who has never time to capture it, almost out of his mind. At one moment the slopes of the fells will be smothered in grey cloud, and a few moments afterwards they will be there in the sunlight, looking like magic carpets. No other place I have ever seen offers such an ever-changing panorama and pageant of colour and light." Whew!

Into mind, as I prepared to fulfil my appointment to speak to the artists at Sedbergh, came the two Reginalds of Upper Wharfedale. There was Reginald Smith, who mixed whisky with the water he used when painting in frosty weather. He contributed paintings and drawings to the first edition of Halliwell Sutcliffe *The Striding Dales*. Reginald was drowned at the Strid in 1934.

Reginald Brundrit, a native of Liverpool who opened a hillside studio near Grassington, in Upper Wharfedale, nearly broke the bank account of the fledgling *Dalesman* when he claimed £25 for his painting on wood, a painting which was damaged when being returned to him by post. A flamboyant character, on being elected Associate of the Royal Academy in 1931, he hired an elephant and its mahout from a circus and was borne in triumph down Piccadilly, arriving at the RA dinner to blasts on a trumpet. His portrait of Fresh Air Stubbs, a Grassington character, was exhibited at the RA in 1934.

James Arundel, of Bradford, sent his men across angry seas to paint lighthouses. James was a much-respected artist who tempted us at the *Dalesman* by offering on free loan the expensive sets of printing blocks. We reproduced his study of the River Aire at Cottingley. It was somewhat streaky but its large size and colourful nature brightened up the centre pages of the magazine. A reader who did not care for "modern art" sent to us a postcard on which she had written:

Aire river? Nay, nivver.
But it maks no matter,
For I can't see t'watter.

A man who loved the scraggy bits of landscape at the edge of the moors was Fred Lawson,who adopted Wensleydale and commended its beauty in quick sketches and majestic paintings, mainly in watercolour, with a strong folk element. Fred had visited Castle Bolton in 1910 for a month's holiday with his friend George Graham. He liked the dale so much he did not want to leave. In due course, he married Muriel Metcalfe, a much younger person who was an artist in her own right.

She recalled that when she first knew him, Fred was a slim, neat man who impressed everyone who knew him because he was a magnificent swimmer. "His hands were small and I was fascinated to see him using them when drawing or painting. He was inspired and did not rely on a set method of painting...Fred was very much himself; the lines flowed...He loved wildness and the snow."

On the day Fred proposed to her, he was painting the fair at Leyburn. "He loved the colour, movement and excitement of fairgrounds, which were set up in the Dales on the old feast days. I sauntered up the town and there he was, just finishing his picture, putting it down carefully so that nobody would tip it over. He had brought his old briar pipe out of his pocket to have a smoke. He leaned against a Town Hall window sill. I was just 18 years old, but we talked as equals for a minute or two. In the background, the roundabout was operating, the music blaring. Fred just looked at me and said: 'Will you marry me?' Just like that. He was absolutely straight. And, of course, I said yes."

Fred was the most unpretentious artist I met. When painting, he donned an old jacket and was sometimes muffled up in sacks. A battered hat protected his head from the vagaries of Dales weather. His home at Castle Bolton was also his studio and art gallery. He sold his paintings for next to nothing. Fred contributed regularly to our maga-zine *Northern Review*, which we published for several years. He wrote pretty well as he spoke and in 1948, in a wistful footnote, stated: "I don't know how you are going on with the weather. But I am getting very little done. It rains every day."

Fred had a regular series in *The Dalesman*. Each month, he sent a scribbled letter and hastily drawn picture. Our readers loved to see them. When I queried what I had taken to be Fred's first abstract draw-ing, accompanying one of his letters, he replied: "Nay – it's a bit o' plaster on the wall in our outside privvy [toilet]."

Herbert Royle lived simply in his cottage home at Nessfield, not far from Ilkley. His companion was a grey parrot. They subsisted without the benefits of electricity or piped water. He was something of a night-bird, working in a field-edge studio to the strains of classical music that emanated from records played on a gramophone. He painted his way through a partial stroke, exchanging his old bike for one which was equipped with a small engine.

Dales weather is transient. An artist must work quickly and confi-dently to capture its moods. My favourite Dales artist, Constance Pearson, who died at Malham in 1970, invariably painted outdoors, using brushes that never held pure colour and keeping water in a screw-top honey jar. Constance, who was born in Leeds in 1886, attended art college and took a teaching post in Cornwall. She returned to the North to marry an art teacher, Sidney Pearson, and they spent their latter days in a cottage at Malham.

Constance's paintings related not just to place but to season and time of day. She masterfully captured the "soft" days on the fells. While seeking subjects, she travelled through Wharfedale and Wensleydale by bus and left the idea of going home precariously late. The paint of her latest picture was usually still wet as she rushed to catch the last bus. Paul Holmes, the first warden at Malham Tarn Field Centre, commissioned from Constance two large collages representing the Dales. They are to be seen hanging above the main staircase of Tarn

House. In her paintings she "froze" life in Malham at an interesting stage in its development. Arthur Raistrick, a great friend of the Pearsons, commented: "They show life in a real Dales village. It's gone now. We'll never see its like again."

The same might be said of the art work of Marie Hartley who first, with Ella Pontefract, then – following Ella's death – with Joan Ingilby, has chronicled Dales life and industry at a crucial stage of evolution. Marie painted in all weathers, usually applying oil paint to hardboard and working quickly and fluently. Her winter studies were sometimes achieved with layers of clothing to insulate her against the cold and with mittens to give partial protection to her hands.

Few natives of the Dales achieved celebrity as artists. Joan Hassell, one of our most outstanding wood engravers, who retired to Malham, had spent most of her life in London, illustrating books for leading publishers. I met her at her home, Priory Cottage, in Malham on a day when winter sunlight, as intense as a searchlight beam, probed every crack and cranny in the living room and everything was seen with the clarity I associated with Joan's work. She first visited Malham in 1932. "It was just like falling in love. I have never been the same since." She worked in the English tradition of engraving and retired to the village in 1977. Among her visiting friends was the distinguished biographer, Margaret Lane. They had worked on Margaret's classic biography of the Brontes.

Joan showed me what she called her Work Barn, which was flavoured by apples. A large hand press, made in 1832, was still in working order. She was using engraving tools that she bought in 1931. There was a gentle swish as she applied the inker to a wood engraving. She carefully positioned a piece of Basingswerke parchment. The old press thwacked as pressure was applied. She peeled from a block of incised wood the study of a hedgehog. She handed the engraving to me and it is one of my most treasured possessions.

The most widely-known of our artists was Joshua Armitage of Hoylake, alias Jos, alias IONICUS, who had done much work for

London publishers and for *Punch*. Answering the door on a dowly [gloomy] day during the monsoon of 1953, we came face to face with Jos, who was wearing stylish clothes, with suede shoes on his feet – hardly the right wear for the fell-country of Yorkshire.

He had arrived in Clapham in response to a commission by *Punch* to illustrate an article on caving. He set off up Ingleborough looking for caves he might sketch. Finding little more than rock, drizzle, mist and mud, he came to us for the loan of pictures of caves on which he might base his work. A batch of photographs was found and, with Yorkshire enterprise, we asked him to provide a cover picture for the magazine. It was the start of a 46-year-long association with Ionicus. He provided us with covers for 16 years, creating at the same time an imaginary Yorkshire dale (Ghylldale) and peopling it with a fascinating bunch of dalesfolk.

The covers were not only artistically pleasing but offered wry social comments. Typical of his work is the picture of a Bohemian type of artist at work in an attractive little Dales village. As he mixes more paint on his palette, having already littered the ground with spent tubes and a bottle that had held something stronger than lemonade, four local men are looking over his shoulder at the work in progress. One thoughtfully rubs his chin as he tries to make sense of – a colourful abstract! My personal friendship with Ionicus continued up to recent death. He was 84 years of age and still busy with his art work.

Ernest Forbes, one of my favourite Yorkshire artists, was not specifically of the Dales but the files of *The Dalesman* contained splendid examples of his work. Ernest, a newspaper cartoonist, tall, handsome, athletic, was one of a coterie of artists associated with Edmund Bogg, the Leeds man who from the 1890s through to the 1920s was a populariser of the Yorkshire Dales through books which were highly romantic in appeal, illustrated by his art-loving friends.

In the early 1930s, *The Yorkshire Post* invited Ernest to tour the county and portray the cathedral cities, market towns and villages. He did so memorably in a series called *This Mellowed Shire*. At Bolton Priory, in

Wharfedale, he was intrigued by some of the names on the old roll, including Adam Blunder, Simon Paunche, Richard Drunken, Tom Noght and, most enchantingly, Whirle the Carter. The last-named was one to conjure with. "That he fetched the dolium of wine from Hulle there can be no doubt and doubtless he attended the weekly 'pandoxation' when the ale was brewed; a beserker breed of man, quick tempered, but great company, and whirling mightily in battle."

Hawes was to Ernest Forbes "a rugged, straggling, thrown-about looking place; built of stone; and with cobbles that harass the feet." In Craven, he met John Coates, of Malham Moor, and heard that when the Morrison estate was sold he had bought three farms. He and his son farmed two of them but it was difficult to get suitable labour. Despite unemployment, "they won't stand for more than eight hours a day; and that's no good in a lambing season."

One of four Marts.

Gone to Ground

The beauty of the Dales is far more than skin deep. The hills are honeycombed with natural shafts and galleries, some with memorable names – Hurtle Pot (its sides smothered in glacial clay), Lost Johns' (there were two of them), Navvy Noodle Hole, Pippikin Pot and Bull Pot of the Witches. The hills are riddled with mine workings, some of which extend from one dale to another. Here and there, shafts remain open, or have a light fence around them, a deterrent to jay-walking farm stock.

My most unforgettable experience was the first time I descended into the main chamber of Gaping Gill. Sitting in a bosun's chair, which was connected with a winch, I felt like a spider on a thread. The descent of 340ft took less than 20 seconds. Standing on a shingly floor, with the hissing of water breaking the silence, I looked upwards to where the head of the shaft was like a rent in the roof of a shattered cathedral. Potholers scattered about the vast chamber looked like glow-worms, though the light was at the other end of their anatomy.

We at *The Dalesman* knew virtually everyone who was potholing – and we published accounts of their discoveries. Nowadays, caving magazines tend to be so fact-laden they are akin to telephone directories. In those days, there was scope in the several club journals for imaginative writing. A potholer who narrowly escaped injury was seen trotting down a chamber "with a boulder half the size of Leeds Town Hall trundling behind him."

Tom Lord, called to use explosives to extend a cave system near Malham, was reported to have entered the hole, stiff-legged, grumbling about his aches and pains – and, having lit the fuse, to have leapt out like a spring rabbit in case there was any air in the packing. Tot, who left school at the age of 13, became a greengrocer, in the family business, but was indifferent to this work, preferring the life of a dealer and developing his archaeological skills.

Tot looked every inch a countryman. He was well-built, with a brick-red complexion. He dressed in a tweedy suit with plus-fours and he donned a trilby hat. His walking stick had a stubber at one end so that on his Dales jaunts he might probe the mole-heaps for microliths and other traces of Early Man.

Tot's collection of cave "finds" attracted wide attention. It began in the 1920s with a regular gathering of friends in one of a range of out-buildings in Upper Settle where his father had killed pigs and which became a repository for bits and pieces of furniture picked up in sales.

Tot Lord.

The six friends called themselves the Pigyard Club. To Arthur Raistrick, of Armstrong College, Newcastle, who became an honorary member, the building was a cal-oil [gossiping place].

Arthur first met Young Tot at Settle in 1924, when he (Arthur) was taking WEA classes on prehistory. It was here that Tot developed his passion for "bones and things". Tom Dugdale, who as a young man knew Tot when the Pig Yard Club met in its original home, told me the room was eventually furnished with a table and seats from old cars which Tot bought for scrap. Other bits and pieces of cars – lamps, horns and objects in brass or chrome –adorned a ledge that ran around the room. What remained of the cars was incinerated on some nearby waste ground to recover solder that was used liberally in car manufacture. The solder and associated muck were heated in a container over a bucket which contained a coke fire. When the impure material had been removed, the pure solder was poured into baking tins for sale.

Tot eventually lived in Town Head, a run-down mansion with a garden over-run by weeds and cats. On a verandah, which gave his home something of the flavour of a film-set for a Somerset Maugham story, Tot loved to sit, not far from where the skull of an elephant reposed. When Tot was not dealing, he was usually leafing through old issues of *Country Life*. I think he fancied himself as a squire.

My caving career began in Bruntscar Cave, which is part of the drainage system of Whernside. The career ended in Alum Pot, which was also known as The Mouth of Hell. Bruntscar, said Norman Thornber, one of the celebrities of the potholing world, described it as "a former show cave". I did not question its accessibility, for Norman was the author of *Pennine Underground,* a book we published listing the underground systems and what might be found in them.

As we reached Bruntscar Farm, the owner of which was known to Norman, he was suffering from stomach pains and felt he ought not to join me and A N Other in the exploration. It was in the days when potholers wore their oldest clothes and ex-army tin hats. Their boots were usually old, preferably with some holes in them. Nearly every underground adventure was attended by wet feet and I might let the water remain in my boots and, having warmed it up, let it continue to warm me, or give it a chance to drain.

The mouth of Bruntscar was as wide as a yawn but soon we found the roof was coming so low we had to crawl, which was a knee-wracking experience. We entered a small chamber, into which the beck was pouring, and had to breast the waterfall to clamber into a passage beyond. On we pressed, ducking under limestone formations, and with an uneasy feeling that the water level was rising and carrying yellowish suds, presumably from disturbed peat. We must retreat.

We did so at speed. When the the small chamber was reached, I sat in the water and, for a short time, my body was damming the stream. I felt it rising up my back. I leapt down, followed by half a ton of water. At home, I became Settle's first streaker. My wife opened the back door of the house, I stripped quickly in the garden and dashed indoors, heading directly for a hot bath.

The problem with Alum Pot was that having got to the bottom, I had difficulty with a big pitch on the way out. The gravitational pull was in my favour as I descended ladders. I reached the sump, an insignificant, scum-covered pool, where the waters gather before beginning a subterranean journey of one and a-half miles, passing *beneath* the Ribble to reappear at Tarn Dub, on the other side of the valley. Having gone as far as I could, I had the indignity of being double-lifelined and shot up like a cork drawn from a bottle.

When Mabel Sharp asked me to first-foot, I went underground. Carrying a torch, I "let the New Year in" at the White Scar cave system in Chapel-le-Dale. Mabel managed the cave for her family. She was superstitious, explaining that this was because she was the daughter of a seafarer. For perhaps 10 years, on the first day of January, I pandered to that superstition, travelling to White Scar in varying weather conditions, but mainly ice and snow.

No one must precede me. For good measure, I must enter the paybox to wish the enterprise well. My first-footing took me on a traverse in the damp and chilly underworld as far as the first waterfall. I never felt to walk alone, being aware that many people had gone before me at other times of the year. A dummy figure, lying flat out in a crevice, with an inch or two of space between the head and cave roof, represented the discoverer of White Scar with a typical section of the original cave passage.

It was in 1923 that Christopher Francis Drake Long, who was taking time off from his studies at Caius College, Cambridge, sat on the heights of Scales Moor, looking across Chapel-le-Dale at a dark patch low on the scar. He crossed the dale to investigate and forced a way into what proved to be an extensive cave at the point of debouchure, instead of through the "attic", the usual point of entry.

On those cold New Year ventures, I mused a good deal about Long, who had a short but action-packed life. His first acquaintance with the Pennine underworld was in 1922 when he explored Stump Cross Cavern, on Greenhow Hill, locating an underground lake. He fell out with the owner of Stump Cross when he covered up the approach to the lake and refused to tell him its location. At White Scar, during what was to be the last year of his life, this young man experienced once again the excitement of going where man had not ventured before.

Few people would envy this modern Orpheus his trip into the Underworld by way of a crawl so low he could breathe only when he lay on his back. He negotiated a tight passage partly filled with water and encountered a skeleton that proved to be that of a sheep. After 220ft, he had the joyous experience of breaking through a stalagmitic barrier and went excitedly on to a subterranean lake (subsequently known as Long Stop Lake). He is said to have swum in it with candles fixed to his helmet. Long died on the surface, not in the "bowels" of Ingleborough. He was thought to have taken his own life, from a drug overdose, but some believe his end was even more tragic. He had been taking the wrong medication.

Among the characters of White Scar was a part-time cave guide who had nautical connections. He was bombarded with questions. Asked about the geology, he is reported to have said: "Flagstone and lime-stone – and concrete on the deck." He pointed to a crack on the wall of the cave and said: "That's the famous Craven Fault." A professor of geology pressed a ten shilling note into the guide's hand and com-mented: "You don't know anything about geology, but it's been one of the most entertaining afternoons of my life." Back at the bungalow, there was time for coffee and fruit cake and to make a fuss of Mabel's cairn terrier before departing for another twelve months.

In spring, cushions of sandwort and other lead-tolerant plants, do their best to obscure the wounds of the once-great lead-mining industry of the Dales. The starry white blooms of the spring sandwort, known to miners as leadwort, and the yellow or violet forms of the mountain pansy can stand a pinch of lead in their diet and have invaded the spoilheaps. When, over several years, Matthew Cherry of Gunnerside gave me a conducted tour of the Swaledale orefield, we usually met in the springtime, when the starry petals gleamed for us. They were to be found in profusion at the back of Kisdon Hill and in Gunnerside Gill, off Swaledale. The best show of mountain pansies I saw was at the hamlet of Booze, above Langthwaite, in Arkengarthdale. A friend called the yellow-violet varieties "Mickey Mouse pansies".

Matthew Cherry, who introduced me to Old Gang, paid his first visit in the company of his grandfather, Annas Bill, who led him over the tops from Gunnerside. In "mining time", the moorland trods were well used. Men converged on Old Gang from Gunnerside, Low Row, Healaugh and Reeth. Annas Bill (whose real name was Bill Buxton) told the lad of the unquenchable faith of a miner in his ability to find lead. When lead lore was discovered in abundance, it was cunningly concealed by clay. Then just enough could be brought out of a level to keep up the price that had been fixed with the owner's agent. Lawrence Barker, a member of a family long associated with the Swaledale orefield, was my companion on the dusty track from Surrender Bridge to Old Gang, a track known to the limping heroes and heroines of Mr Wainwright's coast-to-coast walk. One of them, heading west, told me he had just had a disappointment. After walking towards an ice-cream van, he found it was – a mirage!

We stood in what remains of the smelt mill at Old Gang and admired the chimney, which has been restored. We then clambered up the hillside to where the pillars of a peat-house jutted from the moor like ancient molars on a green gum. Almost 400ft in length, and divided into four sections, the peat-house was, in its prime, roofed with timbers and had a thatching of ling. The sides were left open to the drying winds. The "peeat pots" on the moor were dug to a depth of four feet or more but now have silted up and become colonised by that coarse, unproductive grass known as *Nardus stricta*. .

Eventually, I was able to enter the Realm of t'Auld Man – the dark, damp world of the Dales lead-miner. Over the years, in lonely Pennine gills, dozens of man-made galleries had tempted me to enter them. I didn't, of course. T'Auld man has many traps for the unwary. Darkness is absolute. Baulks of wood hold the puss of decay. A few inches of mud and water conceal a rotting board, underneath which is a 50ft deep hole.

At Park Level Mine, better known as Killhope, near the head of Weardale, a visitor might walk in safety, wading in six inches of water while traversing a former horse-level. Part of the mine was opened up and made safe. Galoshes area available so that visitors remain dryshod. With a dozen others, and led by a young but extremely mine-wise young lady, I waded along a passage lined with unmortared stone. The passage was horseshoe-shaped so that any pressure from above simply tightened up the masonry. The members of the party I joined were equipped with hard hats and electric headlights as well as waterproof overshoes.

Our youthful leader told us that this mine was worked from 1853 until 1910, cutting across 14 veins of lead, which meant it was one of the richest sources of lead ore in the land. Before venturing under-ground, I had visited a mine-shop, the sort of place where miners could lodge from Monday to Friday. The upper room had been refur-bished with bunks, forms and a table. A real fire burnt in a grate. Dummy miners "ligged" in bed. A few (stuffed) rats gave an added touch of realism.

As we ventured underground, our guide suggested that we lifted our feet high as we walked. Pumps are used to deal with the water level. After recent heavy rain, it was slightly higher than usual. We moved like automata, with just the sloshing sound of galoshered feet and an occasional yelp from a visitor who had taken aboard some cold water. Our guide talked about the valuable horses, which belonged to the owners, and the sad plight of the miner, who didn't. The horses were cosseted, shod and draped in leather. The expendable worker looked after himself. What matter if he died, weak, pale and retching, while still in his thirties? There were others to take his place.

In a few minutes we were clear of the water and had our first glimpse of lead – part of a vein that was exposed on the roof. The guide produced a piece of lead ore and gave us the hernia-inducing experience of holding it. We saw a small chamber, hewn out by man, with a plank laid on the ground where miners might seat and open their bait [food] tins where it was relatively dry. They extinguished their lights for economy. At a command from our guide, all lights were extinguished and I experienced for the first time for years what used to be known as pitch darkness.

In our progress through the public part of the mine, we saw shafts draped with ladders of rusting iron or rotting wood. The beams from our headlamps picked out the dim forms of dummy miners set up in working postures. Two dummies were positioned as if they were drilling a hole for a charge of "black powder". Another was breaking up material that had been dislodged. Further along the passage we heard a sound simulating that of gunpowder being detonated underground. Periodically we doused our lights to sample the gloomy state of the mine when there was just one candle for illumination – a candle attached by a lump of clay to the wall of a chamber.

When I had a feeling that our trip was coming to an end, we turned a corner to enter an enormous cavern, hewn out by miners. Most of the space was occupied by a waterwheel which turned with a hissing sound as it was fed with water from above, the water being carried away in wooden troughs. It was this water we had waded through in the level. We emerged, blinkingly, into a dale that was being swept by rain. In the Realm of t'Auld Man, we had at least enjoyed the blessings of a good roof over our heads.

Sacred Places

A dalesman who had never been baptised told me that on the appointed day the horse took fright. "We nivver got to t'church. Mother said it must have been an omen. She never bothered after that." Most people were baptised and grew up fearing God and worrying about what the neighbours would say if they did any work on the Lord's Day.

Sunday in the Dales was notable for its long, unwritten list of don'ts. It was a day for local children to go to Sunday School or twiddle their thumbs. The adults restricted their activities to essential work. Even the sparrows seemed disinclined to chirp. Anyone who hung out washing half-expected to hear a booming voice of rebuke from above the clouds, as in one of Mr de Mille's biblical epics. Or perhaps a thunderbolt would fall and singe the clothes.

There's Methodist in my madness. My grandfather and father were local preachers. So was I, for 40 years. When, at the start, I showed nervousness in a Dales vestry before the service, a steward remarked: "Nay, lad – we should be freightened o' thee. Not thee of us!" I came off the Plan partly because Conference adopted a much higher standard than Christ and insisted that those preachers who had not passed exams should take them – or cease to preach. That would have dessimated the disciples. In modern times, at the stroke of a pen, rural Methodism lost power and appeal.

Most of the Dales auxiliaries, who did not cost Methodism a penny, were hill farmers, characters to a man, some from remote holdings, whose "thee's" and "thou's" were derived from t'Good Book. Their extempore preachers were apt to be repetitive and, when preaching, they were just getting into their mental stride after 20 minutes, but they spoke from the heart and from experience – to people they knew.

My old granny said of a parson with a string of degrees behind his name: "Yon fellow teaches, not preaches." The old-style preachers, those "sweet singers of Zion", bolstered our hopes, stoked up our fears and had a no-holds-barred approach to religion which would be refreshing nowadays, when there is little faith and hardly any constraints.

I still take services – now and again – at little country chapels. One of them is Harrop, tucked away in a quiet part of Bowland and reached along a gated cul de sac. At Harrop, which is now an independent chapel (Methodism had wanted to close it), the congregation is composed mainly of farm folk; the organist plays a harmonium and on cold days a fire glows in an open grate. Afterwards, the fellowship is sustained over a cup o' tea at the nearest farmhouse.

At Timble, in the Washburn Valley, where I was invited to conduct a harvest festival, candles and oil lamps augmented the feeble daylight and the hymn-singing was accompanied by a lady who strummed the keys of a battery-operated Yamaha. At Mount Zion, Tosside, a chapel of the Old Independency which is now open for worship but four times a year, I occupied a pulpit so lofty it was like being on the bridge of a small coaster. In the centre of the chapel glows a huge coke stove. It is sometimes white-hot in the gloom. Years ago, the bride at a wedding walked so close to the stove, her veil was frizzled.

My first professional association with the Anglican church was as a child. I was baptised at Holy Trinity, Skipton. When I became a journalist at the *Craven Herald*, I went to church professionally – to collect the names of mourners at funerals. In those days, the Editor constantly mentioned that "names sell papers". I spent hours standing in chilly porches intercepting mourners who, crow black in their attire and with faces that looked to have been set in mortar, gave me their names in whispers. A few presented me with printed cards.

These same people later formed an animated crowd at the funeral tea which, in true Dales style, featured ham. "Aye, lad, we buried 'im wi' 'am." Funeral teas were apt to be livelier than wedding breakfasts.

Back at the office, I would type the names I had gathered. They would be added to the obituary, which was already in type. It ended customarily with a catch-line, MORE TO COME – a reminder to the printers not to overlook the funeral details, which must be added. The catch-line should always be removed. Once, it remained and subscribers were startled to read that Mr So-and-So was survived by a wife and two daughters, MORE TO COME.

The Dalesman did not print obituaries as such. With each issue prepared weeks in advance of publication date, we lacked the topicality. A notable person would have one or two paragraphs in the Diary devoted to his of her achievements. Churches were often mentioned in the magazine because over the years they had become a repository of interesting objects and inscriptions. They were like rural museums. Their most distinctive contents were mentioned in local guides. Most Dales churches, being extremely old, smelt of dampness and foisty hymn books.

Monasteries fascinated me. At Bolton Priory, one of the old-time Rectors regaled me with ghost stories, including hearing the tap-tap of sandalled feet, and a doctor with a cottage up Wharfedale reported that early one morning he saw ghostly monks at the roadside as he passed Bolton Hall. At Fountains Abbey, by the Skell, I was shown the Green Man. In summer, the abbey - now the jewel in the crown of the National Trust properties in the Dales - rises grey and majestic amid a thousand shades of green.

The mysterious Green Man pointed out to me is thought to be about 500 years old. He occupies a cramped position at the apex of a window in the Chapel of the Nine Altars. I would look at him for minutes on end – then shudder. He has a wild, some say evil, expression, and is not the sort of effigy one would expect to find at a Cistercian abbey, dedicated to high thinking and simple living.

The tradition he represents may hark back to Celtic paganism and to legends of small, secretive beings. In Ireland, they eventually became leprechauns, the "little green people", who doubtless had some cousins in Yorkshire. Was the figure at Fountains Abbey carved to scare off evil spirits? He certainly scared me, with that wild look and with branches of vine (or could it be oak?) growing from his mouth, framing his face with leaves.

Two men I met who had more than a passing interest in the Green Man were Howard Strick, one-time warden at Grantley Hall and organiser of many varied educational courses, and Guy Ragland Phillips. Each has gone to his reward, as a Methodist would say. Howard, who had a passion for the medieval period, introduced archery to Grantley and in his leisure time enjoyed looking for traces of the Green Man. At Ripon, he found what he called The Green Batman. Long before an American devised a cartoon figure called Batman, the "caped crusader", a woodcarver at Ripon decorated a misericord in the cathedral choir stall with a figure which looked to Howard Strick like a Green Man carved upside-down. The little face had, indeed, become that of a bat, hence the inversion. It dated from the 13th century.

Guy, who spent some of his retirement years in Settle, had an imaginative mind and a curiosity about ancient times when humankind worshipped the goods of natural features like hills, woods and rivers. They also paid homage to the spirits to be found in wells, as at Giggleswick, where – Guy thought - St Alkelda was more likely to be an old spirit of the well rather than a Saxon princess. One element of her name is "keld", which meant a spring.

A romantic image of Alkelda as a Saxon princess was set in stained glass. She was also shown being throttled by heathen women, but by the serene look on her face did not seem to mind. At Middleham, in Wensleydale, which has the only other church dedicated to St Alkelda, I made a point of seeking out some older stained glass of the saint being throttled.

My favourite church is tucked away at the head of Wharfedale. Hubberholme, with its yew trees and mini-forest of tombstones, many relating to the Bell family, contains some modern stained glass featuring a 16th century carpenter, William Jake. This ensures he is still beavering away with his plane as he fettles [mends] the rood-loft, a medieval survival in this remote spot. The impulse behind providing the elevated loft, with its altar and crucifix, might have been to enhance the sense of mystery and to curb any tendency of the flock towards over-familiarity with sacred things.

The loft should have been removed in 1571 when an edict went out from York that such connections with the Old Faith should be destroyed. The dalehead was then part of York Diocese. No one in authority appears to have travelled as far as this hamlet to check that the rood-loft had been wrenched out. Or could it have been that the rood-loft came from somewhere else and Jake had the job of trying to make it fit? A former vicar, Harry Isherwood, studied marks on the stonework and believed that, over 400 years ago, this Dales craftsman fitted the loft the wrong way round.

When I last called at the Vicarage in Kirkby Malham, it was on a matter of *grave* concern. The parish church of Malhamdale, known as the Cathedral of the Dales, stands on a spot where Christians have worshipped for 1,000 years. The word "kirkby" is from the Danish, meaning "church place". The grave that concerned me is marked by a tall marble cross, from the base of which comes a flow of water.

I wanted to refresh my memory of the story behind this unique "water" grave. The vicar, who then was Barry Newth, had often been asked about it. He told the story to a few million television viewers when the church was celebrating its 500th birthday. The story goes that Colonel and Mrs John Harrison, of Airton, were separated for long periods because of John's frequent service with the Army overseas. Helen, the wife, with a touch of Victorian whimsy, decided that as water had separated them so often in life, so it should in death. She arranged that the streamlet, which runs through the grave plot, should be the boundary between their final resting places. Helen died in 1890 and was buried on the south side of the stream. John outlived her by 10 years. When the grave-digger came to excavate his portion of the plot, his spade struck impenetrable rock. "So, after all that had been said

131

and done," said the vicar, "they had to be buried together."

As a small boy, being taken by rail from Skipton to Morecambe, I stared in astonishment at a domed building at Giggleswick. Someone in the carriage mentioned that it was an observatory but though I looked until my eyes prickled with fatigue I could not see a telescope protruding from it. Much later, I was aware I had been looking at the chapel of Giggleswick School, perched on a gritstone knoll. I had long been familiar with the interior and, in 1997, attended a special centenary service of this gift from Walter Morrison, which was to commemorate the diamond jubilee of Queen Victoria.

It is said to have been designed to fit the landscape. Hardly. The chapel is an impressive building and local people are fond of it, but it has the visual effect of an exclamation mark. When the Giggleswick schoolboys transferred their attention from the parish church to the new chapel, a villager remarked: "Why do they want to go building a heathen temple up there for?"

Morrison specified a dome because he had admired such a feature during visits to Palestine. The millionaire did not believe in "middle men" and he fixed the site when he visited the gritstone knoll with his architect, T G Jackson, and the joiner, Thomas William Brassington. Impulsively, the donor plunged the tip of his umbrella into the ground where the building was to stand. The Duke of Devonshire laid the foundation stone on October 7, 1897. Into the chapel went stone of several hues. The walls were of local gritstone, faced externally up to the plinth with yellow sandstone brought from Idle, Bradford. Above this level was a facing of red sandstone from Lazonby, in the Eden Valley.

Russell Harty, a former teacher at Giggleswick who achieved national fame as a television presenter, called the place "this incongruously grand chapel". (One of the other masters likened it to a jelly mould). For one of his Christmas programmes, Russell was televised as he listened to the choir rehearsing for the annual carol service. They were singing the Candlelit Carol, which has become a regular feature of the end-of-term carol service at the school.

Ilkley, in Wharfedale.

Viewers of that programme saw the faces of the choristers in the candle glow and a camera revealed the finely decorated underside of the dome. Myriad pieces of mosaic each the size of a sugar lump gleamed and glistened in the strong light. The dome creates an echo when the chapel is empty. If every pew is occupied, the sound has a pleasant resonance, as Harry Secombe discovered when he joined the chapel choir to sing in *Highway*, a series of religious programmes featuring hymns.

I had a modest share in bringing him to the chapel, for the programme dealt mainly with the Settle-Carlisle railway, following a suggestion I made to Border Television. It so happened that when my letter reached Border, one of its executives was about to set off for London – to discuss future programmes in the *Highway* series.

During the 1939-45 war, when a blackout was operating and no naked light was to be shown from buildings after dark, the carol service was held in darkness. The cost of providing light-proof covers for the chapel windows would have been prohibitive. The headmaster, E H Partridge, and the second master, Leonard Dutton, visited the chapel after dark, leaving two lighted candles on the floor of the chancel. They then walked outside to see the effect. The chapel appeared to be glowing like a beacon.

The service took place with just one light – a small torch, held by Mr Partridge when reading passages of Scripture. Charlie Cresswell, of the works staff, was stationed outside, having been instructed to raise the alarm if he heard approaching aircraft. This was not being melodramatic. German bombers regularly passed over the area on their way to Liverpool or Barrow-in-Furness.

A welcome wartime visitor was Roger Quilter, the composer, who was taken to the chapel by Jack Brassington. His most vivid memory was of a chat he had with one of the maintenance men, Thomas Thistlethwaite, known widely as "Tommy Apple". He was so engrossed in his conversation with Quilter that he forgot his school duties. When, later that day, a communion service was held, it was seen that a sweeping brush had been left on the altar.

Philip Curtis, a former chaplain of the school, was fond of recalling when he paid his first visit, to be interviewed by the headmaster. He arrived at Giggleswick station and walked into the village. As he reached the imposing gateway to the Workhouse, he presumed he had arrived at the school and turned in. He knocked on the door and asked if the Headmaster was in residence. The door-keeper said: "Not yet".

Now and again, I would meet Malcolm Skidmore, whose fine voice has lapped itself round many a Biblical text as a local preacher and has also, for 40 years, been employed to good effect as an auctioneer. He developed chronic laryngitis that eventually curtailed, but did not not entirely stop, these activities. To talk with Malcolm is to be transported back to t'auld days.

Half a century ago, at Askrigg Moor chapel in Wensleydale, Malcolm (aged 15) conducted the service and gave what he thought was a conscience-stirring sermon. There were four people in the congregation and three of them were local preachers. When the lad had left the pulpit, one of the preachers, whose name was Minnie Dinsdale, shook him by the hand and said: "It's just what THEY need here." Malcolm laughs at the recollection of a little old lady sitting in chapel thinking of all the good the preacher's message was doing to the others.

When he took his first service while "on trial", he had the company of a cattle dealer who would subsequently report to the local preachers' meeting on how he fared as a preacher. As they returned to the car at the close of the service, he said to Malcolm: "Were you reading that prayer tonight?" Malcolm confessed that he was, having written it out and spoken it with one eye shut and the other open. Said the old preacher: "I'll give thee a bit o' free advice, lad. In future, when thou prays, pray from t'heart, not from a bit o' paper." It was the last time Malcolm used notes.

Arriving a little late for one preaching appointment, he found the congregation had begun to sing the first hymn. "I went marching up into the pulpit. A steward said: 'Sit down'. He spoke with such a stern voice, I thought I was going to get into trouble, but he said: 'We can't keep the Lord waiting...What are your expenses?'" Malcolm indicated there would be no expenses.

At the end of the service, as the steward accompanied Malcolm back to his car, they walked through the churchyard. Said the steward, with great reverence: "Ponder awhile and think of the great company we are amongst." During the following week, an envelope arrived. It contained a half-crown book of stamps and a little letter of thanks.

The Long Drag

I was afflicted by Settle-Carlilitis at an early age. This complaint, for which there is no known cure, relates to the Settle-Carlisle railway, the most dramatic in Britain. The Midland built a first-class, all-weather line that has a devil-may-care attitude to the landscape, with its formidable viaducts, cuttings, embankments and tunnels.

My godfather, Ted Boak, of Skipton, was one of the men who flogged the sooty locomotives up the Long Drag, on a ruling gradient of 1 in 100. Ted kept unsociable hours in the days when a knocker-up rapped a pole on the windows of those on the duty roster and brought them from their beds with the sleep-mist still in their eyes. He told me of crossing Ribblehead viaduct in a westerly gale, when he and his firemen snuggled down for a minute or so as the wind howled about them.

There were moments of high comedy, such as when a lengthman at Garsdale persuaded him to drop off some coal at their remote little hut and a particularly large cob was so well aimed it burst open the door and caused consternation among men gathered around the stove. An old lady with a lineside cottage placed her unwanted bottles on a wall-top as a tempting target for the footplate men on passing trains, who threw coal – and kept her in fuel throughout the year.

My introduction to the Settle-Carlisle came during a visit to Ribblehead station, which stands in as wild a spot as you might imagine. In 1998, the main building was restored and no longer does the wind moan between shattered slates. New guttering and downspouts deal with a rainfall that averages 70 inches a year. When I came across Ribblehead in the 1950s, I admired the station's vaguely gothic style and its "frontier feel". It's the place where the railway begins its high fell-wandering.

Garsdale, on the Settle-Carlisle.

Ribblehead had a harmonium in the waiting room and a wind-vane on the roof. The little station combined its railway role with that of a church and weather station. The first stationmaster I knew was Martin Elliott. It was a time when a stationmaster was a much-respected member of the community. He wore a smart uniform with "scrambled egg" on the neb of his cap. Martin was at Ribblehead in January, 1954 when a rain gauge was installed. That same year, a total of 109 inches of rain were recorded.

Bill Sharpe, a successor as stationmaster, had an office with a wall-chart of the various cloud formations. He used the telephone hourly to transmit a coded message about the weather to the Air Ministry. At a time when over 100 steam-hauled trains passed during a working day, and some of them stopped with passengers and goods, he scarcely had time to brew himself a cup of tea. He was also the lamp man, venturing forth to replace the paraffin containers at local signals.

The waiting room was a social centre. Monthly services were conducted by the vicar of Ingleton. At another time, dancing took place to music provided via gramophone records. The strains of Victor Sylvester's band were heard above the moan of the wind. Ribblehead was at its busiest when the quarry was active, reducing limestone to dust as fine as face powder, and when farmers delivered or collected farm stock, which was accommodated in the cattle pens.

A ganger, who lived at one of the Salt Lake Cottages, remembered when the Royal Train, carrying the Queen Mother, was due when some cattle broke free and ran down the track. They were collected with only minutes to spare. The same ganger, during the war, was crossing Ribblehead viaduct when he saw a British bomber fly straight into Whernside.

When the Home Guard was active, and members regularly "kept guard" on the viaduct, it was customary for men to meet before and after a spell of duty at the waiting room of Ribblehead station. A young man was asked if his rifle had been cleared of ammunition. He nodded and, to demonstrate, pulled the trigger. There was a deafening explosion. A bullet sang as it went through the ceiling and slates. The damage was visible to those who knew about it for years afterwards.

Occasionally, from Garsdale, I took the Wensleydale line. Once, being the only passenger, the driver invited me to travel on the footplate. He dropped me off at Aysgarth. The Bradford-Hawes express, which operated at that time, was known as Bonnyface to the permanent way men. The name related, I was told, to an ugly permanent way inspector who travelled at half fare because the top part of his body was usually sticking out of the carriage window as he checked on the work of the men.

A more reasonable explanation is that when the train began its return to Bradford the workers knew it was almost time to knock off work for the day. Even though its face was streaked with soot, it was bonny to those who had been working hard and long.

Garsdale, like Ribblehead, was a social centre, with a library in the waiting room and whist drives and dances being held in the Tank House, beneath the huge iron tank. I heard that at the time of the conversion, just after the 1914-18 war, material used in the munition factories was being sold cheaply, The Garsdale men visited all the local sales with £25 raised by a special dance held in the village school. Some quality timber was purchased for the dance floor. The £25 also covered the cost of a gramophone, piano and lamps.

The place was cheerfully decorated. Refreshments at dances were served in a wheel-less railway carriage of Midland ancestry set endways on the Tank House. The coach held two long tables and some chairs. There was "a bit of a kitchen, with a coke stove for heating water." "Sixpenny hops" were held right up to the coming of television, when people began to stay at home on Saturday evenings.

Some of my best friends in the Dales have been railwaymen and their families, especially those with homes and jobs at remote parts of the line. I had not been at *The Dalesman* long before Settle-Carlitis flared up again and I alleviated it by going to the trackside. George Horner, who first worked in Blea Moor signal box during t'summer of 1953, had some classic tales to tell of the Settle-Carlisle in t'transition period when "they were changing from steam to diesel...At that time you didn't always go by class. You'd ask t'bloke behind: 'What's this divvil got on? Is he a steamer or a diesel?' You had to go against convention and decide which was fastest and which should have the road."

It was George who told me about the Blea Moor chemical toilet, an Elsan, situated in its little wooden hut at the top of the steps. A signal-man who was keen on smoking a pipe usually lit up when he was sitting on the toilet, passing the spent match between his legs into the bucket below. One day, the match was not spent when it was dropped into the bucket and the railwayman was in danger of being grilled when the chemicals set on fire. George added: "That arrangement was newish. A toilet at the old signal boxes was a lile tin shack a few yards away. It wasn't always safe in a real strong wind. I've heard of one tekkin' off wi'a fellow sat theer."

George was one of those who featured in an audio-visual presentation compiled by my old friend Bob Swallow. He dealt largely with folklore. I loaned Bob some tape recordings of railwaymen from my collection. He added some of his own and supplemented them with a breezy commentary. His slides evoked the beauty of the line at all times of day and all seasons of the year.

George told of the inspector, a "whiskery sort of fellow", newly appointed, who "landed up" to Blea Moor "one reight grand bright summer day as he looked round his new parish." He said to George: "I've never been up here before. My, but it's grand. You can see for miles. What a grand spot." George agreed that was so, on a bright summer day. "It's a bit different when t'snowflakes are flying about." The new inspector commented that the men he had met were all the same; they did not think there was another railway to compete with the Settle-Carlisle. After a while, George moved from Blea Moor to

Horton-in-Ribblesdale.

Three years later he met the man again. Now he was traffic inspector on t'snow plough. "He was struggling on his way to Blea Moor. Eventually he made it, then returned with difficulty to Horton, with ice sticking to every whisker on his face. Walking in at the door, he said he'd never come across such conditions." George reminded him of what he'd said. "It's same as any other railway..." The inspector spluttered: "Shut your trap. I know what I said..."

Jim Taylor, stationmaster at Horton, then Settle, created prize-winning gardens at each place by hacking up parts of the platform. "We didn't bother asking about it; we just hacked 'em up and presented it to 'em [authority!] as a *fate accompli*. We won the garden competitions for seventeen years."

Jim, recalling his Horton days, told me the comical tale of a teacake. When a train made an unscheduled halt on the "down" platform, waiting for signal clearance, Jim would stroll across, knowing that whenever a train stopped, for whatever reason, someone was bound to get off. The expresses used to have a dining car and one of the staff was sure to look out and ask why the train was stopping. Jim would explain that "your sparring partners in front are doing badly. You'll be away in a few minutes. By the way, you haven't kept up the old custom. If you are on block and you stop here, you always ensure that the stationmaster, who is invariably on the platform, is presented with a toasted teacake."

The incredulous waiter would say: "Is that right?" He would then dash off and return with a toasted teacake. Jim chuckled and added: "He must have spread the word about, for from that day, whenever an express was held up by a signal and I was on the platform, I was presented with a toasted teacake."

George told of a platelayer who was working between the bridge and the south portal of Blea Moor tunnel. It was a sunny day and in the cutting conditions were terribly hot. They all took their shirts off. "One fellow had hung his shirt over one of the little willow bushes at t'lineside. The look-out man blew his hooter. They stood clear for t'express to go by. As it went by there was a shirt flapping about in t'loco's motions. George tipped off his colleagues down the line, assuring them there wasn't a fella in it.

When the platelayers finished their job, and were walking towards the signal box, each of them bar one had a shirt over his arm. "I thought he must have lost his shirt so I asked him what had happened to it. He said the blooming express gathered it up off t'willow bushes. By gum, he'd be in lumber [trouble] when he got home. What should he tell his wife? George said: "Tell her what happened - that t'express gathered it up off t'willow bushes." He said: "Do you think she'll believe a story like that, man?"

Tony Freschini, resident engineer on the Ribblehead viaduct renovation project, was told, as the work came towards a close, that a coffin was propped up against a parapet. Said Tony: "I thought it must be a joke. I questioned the man who reported it because I would have to climb 100ft up the embankment and then walk across the viaduct to where the coffin was said to be. As I reached the track I could see in the distance that there *was* a something in the refuge. It was a coffin. An arm was hanging out of it."

When Tony got nearer, he saw a silver plate with WALTER written on it. He also noticed that the arm was made of rubber. "I didn't quite know what to expect inside so I flung it open with a shriek. The three people who had followed me fled in terror. The coffin was empty."

It was George who told us about Nancy Edmondson, one of the "railway children" of Blea Moor. During 1939, said Nancy, "our dad, John Dawson, was offered and accepted the sub-ganger's post at Blea Moor. The attraction was a tied property, No 1 Blea Moor Cottages, one of a pair of traditional Midland houses." Nancy was then a year old, with two older sisters, Edith 12 and Margaret 10. Water was supplied to the washhouse, outside the property, from the same source that fed the huge water tanks used to replenish thirsty locomotives. Coal came courtesy of firemen's shovels. Lighting was by paraffin and candles.

"Our toilet was a mite primitive – an earth closet at the bottom of the garden. At night, we took a candle, shielding it from the wind with an enamel jug. The toilet was at a draughty spot where the paper didn't always stay put. Later, dad scoffed at our new chemical variant. 'Them as use it can empty it,' he said, promptly departing for a local pothole."

Schooling for Nancy and her sisters involved a one and a quarter mile trek to Ribblehead, from where a bus took them to Chapel-le-Dale and later Settle School. "On a windy day, Margaret and I would load the hems of our waterproofs with small stones so we would not become airborne as we walked under the viaduct. We sheltered behind a pier before making a dash for it. Frequently and against the rules we would walk across the viaduct, where the parapet and our lack of inches meant it was surprisingly sheltered."

The early part of 1947 was amazing. The worst blizzard anyone could remember raged across Blea Moor. "Dad fought a losing battle to keep the points clear. Beyond our house lay a cutting, blocked solid, with a snowplough blocked in its midst. In desperation, a jet engine mounted on a flat truck was brought up the Drag in an endeavour to blow a way through. 'It'll never get up here,' said our dad, sitting on a rail and filling his pipe. Of course, he was right. It stuck in the first minor drift and had to be cut out by prisoners of war.

"All normal services were suspended, so we rode down to Settle on (or rather in) the plough. Not so unusual really. We seemed to ride most places on locomotives. Edith set some sort of record on her wedding day, leaving home, hair in curlers, wedding dress over her arm, bridal transport care of a passing Midland 4F 0-6-0 freight locomotive, which had been brought to an unscheduled stop at the signals. I wonder what the crew were thinking as they deposited her at Ribblehead, where she changed into her finery at the Station Inn prior to the wedding at Chapel-le-Dale."

Nancy's other sister, Margaret, went one better when, going into labour, unexpectedly early, her signalman's husband colleague stopped the up-Thames-Clyde express. "The guard pulled and tugged. Dad pushed and shoved. And several passengers lent a hand. And that just to get her into a carriage. Later, at Skipton, a son was delivered, sound in wind and limb."

My old friend Jim Fishwick, of Hellifield, recounted what happened when a footplate man from a train held up by signals entered the box at Selside when it was manned exclusively by women. "One remark you often heard was: 'Come on – get 'em off!' Whoever said it to a signalman meant 'get the pegs [signals] off.' He would be on mileage work and was anxious to be on his way. This day, when a lady was in charge of the box, a man from Leeds dashed up the steps and said: 'Come on – get 'em off.' She thought he meant something else. She slapped his face and reported him."

My favourite part of the Dales is around the church in Chapel-le-Dale. In this limestone land, the river plays hide and seek in potholes and caves. Trolls inhabit mossy woodland and, just before dawn, scutter back into potholes, the mouths of which are lagged with ransoms, the fleshy plant that most of us call wild garlic. A Victorian courting couple were terrified when they heard a wailing sound from Hurtle Pot, which lies just behind the church, but it turned out to be an indifferent violinist.

The lych gate at St Leonard's Church frames a view of the steep northern side of Ingleborough. John Ruskin, travelling up the valley on a gale-ridden day, marvelled that the mountain could stand without rocking. It was at Chapel-le-Dale that I sensed the heroic side of the Settle-Carlisle – the endurance, in bitter conditions, of workers and their families. The most ornate gravestone in the churchyard is inscribed Job Hirst, who in the 1870s was a sub-contractor during the construction of Batty Moss viaduct, now better known as Ribblehead.

Job's six foot of English ground, on the right when you have passed through the lych gate, is covered by a finely carved stone, one end being surmounted by a stone cross. Job was born in 1815 at

Kirkheaton, near Huddersfield, and his first job was that of stone mason. He turned his attention to the business of building "long bridges of several spans", now better known as viaducts. At Ribblehead, in his prime as a contractor, Job had to organise the quarrying of dark limestone from the bed of the stream in Littledale. Old folk still claim that the immense viaduct was "built on wool", whereas the bases of the piers were laid on concrete over bedrock.

Work on the viaduct progressed from north to south. Job had the immediate assistance of his sons, Walter and Charles Henry. When Walter "came of age" in November, 1872, father provided him with a celebratory supper in the wooden schoolroom at Batty Green. In attendance were about 140 masons and labourers, also some family friends. Job gave his son a gold watch. A month later, Job, aged 57 years, was dead and buried.

He had gone by horse and trap from Ribblehead to Ingleton to collect his men's wages. A blizzard was raging. As he returned to Ribblehead, some villains set upon him and took his money and gold watch, leaving poor Job unconscious at the roadside. When he recovered, he was able to scramble to where his gold watch was dangling from a stile. He regained his horse and trap, but fainted once more. The untended horse brought the trap back to the family lodging. Job's wife found him lying on the floor of the trap and revived him with port. They went to bed. In the morning, she found him lying dead beside her. The doctor said Job had died of an apoplectic fit and that port was the worst drink he could have had.

He was buried in Chapel-le-Dale churchyard where, eventually, the bodies of more than 200 people connected with the dalehead shanty towns were interred. Job's sons completed the work of building Ribblehead viaduct. Now, near pier 13, is a monument to those who laboured during its construction and those who renovated it in recent times. The cost of the renovation equalled in the number of pounds the total cost of the railway in the inflationary 1870s.

Nowt but Scenery

It was a Bradford man, who taken round the Dales by his daughter, commented: "It's nowt but scenery". Dale-country is not as dramatic as the craggy heart of the Lake District, to the north-west. Pennine horizons are generally low. Ridge after ridge, in various shades of grey or blue, lie under a big sky. In gritstone areas, in late summer, the underbellies of the clouds seem to take on a purple hue from the flowering ling.

The Pennine fellsides are rather plain, patterned by drystone walls, with one or two wheezy thorn trees and the odd rowan clinging to the side of a gill. Most of the low land has wall-to-wall ryegrass, ideal for silage, winter fodder for the cattle. The emerald green contrasts with the floriferous fields of the daleheads, where grants are available to preserve the botanical part of our heritage.

Until the unhappy changes in bounty boundaries that took place in 1974, Yorkshire claimed Mickle Fell, on the northern Pennines, as its highest point, 2,591ft. The honour now goes to Whernside, which is basically a ridge. Climb it in mist and it has a series of false-summits. Ingleborough is the most distinctive hill because of its conspicuous flat-top and the glacial valleys around which isolate it. Ingleborough's bold form is visible from Buttertubs Pass, to the east, and from the sands of Morecambe Bay, far to the west. It is in view from South Lakeland. Travellers on the A65, heading north, see the shallow valley of the Ribble and, beyond, Ingleborough, stretching itself languidly across the northern horizon.

Penyghent has a distinctive outline, with a conspicuous band of limestone, where grows the purple saxifrage. I was once looking at a cushion of this plant on a day when the warmth of the rock was melting the snow cover. On that vast hill, I was fascinated to see bees

Bolton Woods, Wharfedale.

looking for nectar. See Penyghent from Dalehead, in the east, and it looks like a marooned whale. From the west, it takes on the appearance of a recumbent lion, with a splendid mane.

The nose-end of Penyghent enhances the view from the Ribble bridge between Settle and Giggleswick. A local philosopher spent so long contemplating that view that someone asked him what great thoughts had been going through his mind. He said: "I was just thinking how much Penyghent resembles an upturned pudding dish."

The hills of the Dales are a vast recreation ground for ramblers, now known as fell-walkers. It is a relatively modern pastime, for although the Yorkshire Ramblers' Club was storming the fells in Victorian times, the main interest of its members was in climbing and potholing. Rambling was an inexpensive occupation for many during the trade recession between the wars. It was then that working class men "discovered" the countryside. They wore rough everyday wear and studded boots. Just after the 1939-45 war, the type of camouflaged capes issued to soldiers were available as surplus equipment and proved ideal for countrygoers.

The Rambler or fell-walker has a leisure time occupation with no age limits. A member of a Dales walking club for veterans achieved fame among his fellows not so much for a heart attack on Ingleborough but because his body was lifted off his favourite mountain by helicopter. My own walking has been mainly with three friends. We call ourselves the Geriatric Blunderers' Club and our motto is "You name it – we've been lost on it." The president is Betty Wainwright, widow of the celebrated AW of guide book fame.

We have trudged far and wide. Of the eastern fells, we consider that Buckden Pike is not much to look at but excels as a vantage point. A J Brown, a walker's writer, ascended the Pike when "a snell wind was blowing" and although the fell was "just a shaggy giant of the early world, a great lump of a mountain", the view from the top was enchanting.

Hearing the sad tale of an RAF plane which crashed here in the

1940s, I climbed the Pike from Starbotton. The lane from Starbotton to the Peat Ground had the gradient of a house roof. Two stretches were signposted "deep bog", which did not deter a dozen well-muddied motor cyclists from enjoying an off-road excursion. Roaring up from Starbotton, they ignored the deepest ruts and carved new courses for themselves across the remaining stretches of grass.

The peaty track was like a skidpan, having soaked up heavy rain and been stirred by boots into a glutinous mass. Now it was my turn to feel guilty at causing erosion. On my crossing of the Peat Ground I viewed cotton grass, the great peat-forming plant of the Pennines, and yellow mountain pansy, shivering in the breeze, defying me to photograph it without getting a blurred image. The leaves of cloudberry were to be seen in a tangle of coarse grasses where, within living memory, there was heather.

Breaking the Wharfedale skyline, I languidly took in the features of moors and little dales, stretching eastward to the Plain of York, beyond which stood the grey-blue edge of the North York Moors. Wildlife was entertaining but sparse. A meadow pipit descended in "shuttlecock" song flight. Its wings and tail feathers were held stiffly outwards. It shared the air space with the skylark, a feathered helicopter. A curlew drawled afar off. Much nearer, a golden plover piped a warning – *tlu-i, tlu-i* – a melancholic sound. For a few moments I felt sad.

Then I heard the call of the Greater Anguished Walker, calling to its mate. The walker was in an area where peat had been boot-beaten into the consistency of Yorkshire pudding mixture. The mate uttered consoling sounds and went to the rescue. Shortly afterwards, a fox came into view. It stared unblinking, even when I was a few yards away. A rambler strolled up to it and rubbed its shiny nose – for luck. As you will have suspected, the fox was not one of the flesh, blood and fur variety. It was fashioned of metal, being a feature on the memorial to five of the six Polish members of a wartime RAF crew who died when their Wellington bomber crashed in this high and lonely spot.

They had been on a training flight in January, 1942. The aircraft hit snowy Buckden Pike a few yards to the south of the summit. All but one man died and he was badly injured. Descending the Pike on all-fours, he saw the tracks of a fox and followed them down the fellside to the hamlet of Cray, where the Parker family were roused and gave what help they could. Hence the symbol of a fox on the cross which forms a memorial to five luckless men. Their memorial is decked with a crucifix and with pieces of the shattered aircraft, concreted into the base. (The bodies of the victims were interred at Newark).

Tan Hill, on the Yorkshire-Durham border, lacks a distinctive shape but is widely known because its inn, at 1,732ft is the most elevated hostelry in the land. Its nucleus dates from the days when thin, high seams of coal were mined. Old folk have told me of the most celebrated landlady, Susan Peacock, who died rather more than 60 years ago. This wispy woman loved "quiet places" and once a year, in spring, went on a shopping jaunt to Darlington.

Susan was born at West Witton, in Wensleydale. At one time she was housekeeper for a Coverdale farmer, and then went into service with a Craven farming family. Her first husband, Richard (Dickie) Parrington, was the licensee of the Cat Hole Inn at Keld before he took over Tan Hill. They had three daughters. When Dickie popped his clogs [died], Susan married Michael Peacock, a roadman born in Arkengarthdale. In the 1930s, t'wireless folk discovered Tan Hill. Susan was persuaded to broadcast, though the wireless did not appeal to her and she said of her husband that "he's not struck on it either."

In May, Tan Hill is the setting for an invasion of Dales farmers and sightseers attending the annual sheep show, at which further entertainment is provided by a brass band. Once, winter lingered into spring and a blustering wind was heavy with rain. Having parked near Tan Hill inn, I had no inclination to leave the car. Extra fame came to this solitary, fell-top pub through an advertisement lauding the effectiveness of a certain make of double-glazed windows. They were so effective, a feather gently fell, untroubled by draughts.

Stand on the outcropping gritstone behind the inn and you see the place in its wild context. The eyes range over immense distances to some of the Pennine giants – to Great Shunner Fell, to High Street and Nine Standards Rigg. Many a Yorkshire cyclist has memories of battling against the wind to reach the inn when it was small and somewhat primitive. Donald Lee, of Keighley - Gig to his many friends – knew Susan Peacock and her husband Michael in the setting of their "mountain home". Gig and a pal were at Tan Hill in the summer of 1929, having travelled from the Aire Valley on a borrowed tandem.

They stopped at Hawes for a snack meal, then crossed the Buttertubs Pass to the upper valley of the Swale. "By t'middle of t'afternoon we were through West Stonesdale and climbing to Tan Hill, where Michael was standing behind the bar." The two cyclists asked for shandies and though it was "out of hours" Michael did not hesitate to serve them. Gig asked him what would happen if the local policeman arrived. Said the barman: "He'll have bin ridin' his bike and will want a pint. If t'bobby can have one, so can you."

Susan's goat was almost as much an institution as Tan Hill itself. The goat met every car that arrived at this remote spot. Susan told visitors her goat liked chocolate. It just so happened that she had a stock of chocolate for sale. Where chocolate was concerned "yon goat is one of my best customers." Donald Lee realised an old ambition when, a year or two after Susan's death, he spent a night at her old home. Michael and his daughter Edna were then running Tan Hill inn.

Donald recalled a high bed, with "brass knobs on". In the tiny bedroom was a water jug and basin for washing purposes. Next morning, he arose and wandered round the inn, meeting no one. He went outside and saw Edna returning with a yoke on her shoulders to support two pails full of water she had drawn from a spring beside the Arkengarthdale road. Such was the origin of the drinking water used at Tan Hill, the highest licensed premises in England.

A favourite hill-top hamlet in Arkengarthdale, a valley where there is a great deal of scenery, is called Booze. From Fremington Edge, a path dips into Slei Gill and runs through an area tormented by lead-mining. The mine in Faggerhill (a Norse name) is said to have had over 25 miles of rails. By Arkle Beck, some 600ft down the hillside, was the entrance to Booze Wood Level, which was driven northward to encounter the profitable Booze Vein. Booze is a group of farms and cottages straddling a fellside. The name is the hamlet's unloveliest aspect. It's supposed to mean "house by the bow or curve". Another theory is that the name is a corruption of the Old English *bowehouse*. Utter this word rapidly a few times and you will find yourself saying "booze". A J Brown, whose writings captured the spirit of the upper dales, noted: "Booze, despite its encouraging name, is about the most teetotal hamlet I have ever explored hopefully, from end to bitter end."

Those who like their environment cosy and well-wooded might follow the Reginald Farrer Trail through the woods of Clapdale, where in spring blobs of colour from rhododendrons in full bloom almost shout to be noticed. Reginald (1880-1920) grew up at Ingleborough Hall in Clapham with a fascination for rock gardening. He gave the wooded gorge the semblance of a Himalayan valley by planting rhododendrons and bamboos. He also introduced rock plants to the cliffs on the eastern side of a lake and is said to have reached inaccessible areas by firing the seeds from a muzzle-loader as his boat drifted by.

Farrer's "rhodies" had become old and leggy in recent times when an old man called Charles Graham devised a scheme to rejuvenate the groves. He reared seeds in an outbuilding at his home at Giggleswick, then distributed young plants in the old haunts. At times, when doing this, he swung from a rope tethered to a tree and used adroit footwork to reach the desired areas.

Reginald Farrer had a passion for the exotic. He kept Siamese cats, to some of which he dedicated books. Farrer was easily moved to emotion in the presence of plants that made a special appeal. When visiting Holden Clough nursery, near Bolton-by-Bowland, he prostrated himself before one of the shrubs.

This astonishing man, who from his boyhood at Clapham had a love of high, remote places, died miserably in the wilds when on a plant-hunting expedition to upper Burma in the autumn of 1920. When he became ill, runners were sent for help. The end came with only a Chinese cook in attendance. His mother, who grieved for him to the end of her life, 17 years later, erected a memorial to him on the terrace at Ingleborough Hall, with the inscription: "He died for love and duty in search of rare plants."

Herriot Fever

The shopkeeper at Leyburn, in Wensleydale, was wondering where all the day-trippers had gone. The market square looked like the film set for *High Noon*. I suggested that as the summer of 1998 had been almost continuously wild and wet, many of the tourists had not even set off from home. She sighed. "Perhaps. But I have this feeling that the pressure has been taken off us. Nowadays, the day-trippers seem to be going to *Heartbeat Country*."

There's a fickle element in tourism, which is a relatively modern phenomenon in the way it caters for vast numbers of people. Yet many people still feel a warm glow around the heart when they think of James Herriot and his Yorkshire Dales – the Dales of the 1930s, just before war brought about profound social changes.

Compared with today, that was an age of innocence. Herriot, in real life Alf Wight the vet, fictionalised much of his work. Why not? To be a good read, a book needs strong characters, with an appropriate number of goodies and baddies. It needs plots that are tense and full of incident. Many people had written about the Dales and made an effort to describe its people and places. No one did it better than James Herriot. The way in which the world took to his work, in its original book form and in films and television series, must have astonished even him.

Alf Wight came in and out of my life at *The Dalesman* over a long period, usually by letter, occasionally by telephone and, on two memorable occasions, face to face. The last time, 1990, was in his attic studio, with Bodie, his Border terrier, snoozing under his chair. Before me, in a bungalow standing in a village near Thirsk, was this quiet-spoken, affable man – a man reared and educated in Glasgow – who had not only transformed the way in which people think of the Yorkshire Dales but had given veterinary science a human face.

I remember him describing to me, in our encounter at his bungalow, some upper dale characters of the old type. They included the "little woman" in a cheerless kitchen, the sort he entered when, having attended to a cow in the shippon, he was invited in for a cup of tea. "The kitchen was a big flagged place. Enormous. You couldn't help but feel sorry for the women who had to work in such a cold, draughty place. The farmer's wife who opened the door might have an apron made of sacking. Sometimes she had clogs on her feet."

The Herriot books have the romance derived from considering a simplistic way of life. It was probably the last time that dalesfolk were truly in tune with the dale-country. They were at the tab-end of a tradition of handwork performed in arduous conditions. Not for Alf the academic's dry notes, with footnotes. His comments on social changes were in story form. He recalled what he did, what he saw and what he heard.

To return to the Dales farmhouse kitchen, he mentioned to me a sight I had half-forgotten, the time when "huge sides of fat bacon hung from hooks driven into the ceiling. You had to duck your head to avoid brushing against them. Bacon was what they lived on. Every time you went into a kitchen, there was this lovely smell of bacon being cooked." The hardiness of the dalesfolk amazed him. When he first knew them, he was in his twenties, yet "I'd see a fellow in his seventies shovelling away in the teeth of a cutting wind. 'It's blowing a bit thin this morning,' he would say. He'd just have a jacket on and I'd a muffler and a heavy overcoat. They were hardy fellows."

Herriot Country, one of those labels devised by the tourist industry which grew apace after Herriot's time, was prompted mainly by the televised tales, set against a backdrop of the northern dale-country, with its bare sheep ridges, its moors and steep-sided valleys. Celebrities are a natural by-product of television. Soon millions of people the world over had augmented impressions of the Dales gained from books with vivid television pictures.

Television has led to the re-drawing of the map of Yorkshire. The county now has its *Summer Wine Country*, a little to the south of the old-established Bronte Country and *Emmerdale Country*, from the series which began as Emmerdale Farm, set originally in Littondale, where many of the early sequences were "shot". *Herriot Country* is the touristy label for the northern dales, mainly Swaledale and Wensleydale and their tributary valleys. *Heartbeat Country*, based on the once-quiet moorland village of Goathland, is the backdrop against which were set the adventures of a rural police constable. The series needed a catchy name. The script-writers ensured the chosen area experienced a serious crime wave for our hero to combat and lots of soppy sequences for us to weep over.

Alas, poor Goathland! What have the filmsters done to you? I recall the village in the 1950s, with its red pantile roofs set against purple moorland and with farmsteads reeking of turf-fires. Among the sheep that ventured from the moors to graze the village greens was Matilda, who dropped and coddled her lambs beside the churchyard wall. The throb of bus engines and tinkle of cash registers have joined the moorland sounds.

The Alf Wight who fell in love with the Dales was an off-comer, a native of Sunderland whose family moved to Glasgow when he was a child. He grew up in a world of bustle and trams. "I'm a city boy," he told me. "Glasgow, a much maligned city, is surrounded by beautiful country. I spent all my boyhood and youth on the Scottish mountains. We used to go camping nearly every week-end."

His first and only veterinary job was in the practice at Thirsk. He had responded to an advertisement and rejoiced in having a job at a time of high unemployment and industrial slackness. His introduction to the "magic land" of the Dales came about when he travelled three times a week from his base at Thirsk to Leyburn, where he assisted Frank Bingham, the local vet, with the tuberculin-testing of cattle.

Frank was a tall, handsome Irishman who, in the books, is referred to as Ewan Ross. He had a Swiss wife and two sons. "Like a lot of the vets of these days, he liked a drink. Many apocryphal tales are told about him. But he was a wonderful chap, one of my favourite men. He was very kind to me." Frank had a car, though some vets were still going about on motor-bikes. "Once I got embedded as his helper with the ordinary tuberculin-testing, he would say: 'Oh, while you're there, just castrate a couple of colts.' Bit by bit I found I was not only a tester but a practitioner in the Dales. And I got to know every nook and cranny - right up to Gayle in Wensleydale and to beyond Keld in Swaledale and away up to the head of Coverdale."

In the early 1940s, farmers were using some methods of treating their stock which were not far removed from Black Magic. "That was probably what motivated me to write a book in the first place. It was a very funny time in veterinary practice." Alf referred to "all those awful old treatments. A cow went down. The farmer would say it had 'a worm in its tail'. The cow couldn't get up, so they cut its tail off. Another farmer kept a billy goat (which stank) in the shippon to prevent contagious abortion. He thought the smell would help cure the complaint. Yet abortion hit a herd only once. Then the animals developed an immunity. The herd was alright next year. The billy goat got the credit."

Alf travelled about the Dales in "a funny old Austin 10". All vets were impecunious in every way. "This car had no heater, of course. The floor was broken and every time I went over a puddle the muddy water would splash up into my face. The windscreen had become so cracked that there were only one or two places I could peer through. Amazingly, it took me on my rounds, up hill and down dale."

There was one terrible period when the brakes did not work. "We couldn't get around to sorting out the brakes, so I drove all over those hilly places without being able to use them. I put a bit in my book about travelling into West Witton from the moor-top and negotiating the terrible hairpin bends, without any brakes on the car. I wouldn't do that now if you gave me a million pounds."

I mentioned to Alf Wight that I never motor through Carperby in Wensleydale without looking at the Wheatsheaf and recalling the story of the Herriots's unusual honeymoon, partly spent tuberculin-testing cows. Alf grinned and replied: "I hadn't a bean in those days." He and his new wife Joan [the Helen of the series] spent part of the time with the livestock. He injected the cows and called out their skin measurements. She jotted down the records. They had been married at Thirsk and arrived in Carperby after dark. None the less, Mrs Kilburn and her niece Gladys were waiting with a hot meal –the first of many memorable meals. "The farmers were aghast that I should spend part of my honeymoon doing vet's work. Yet it was a very good honeymoon and it was cheap!"

The fictitious Darrowby of the Herriot tales has been generally thought of as an amalgam of various places known to its creator. Alf himself told me that Darrowby is a thinly-disguised Thirsk. "It has to be. I was married here. My kids were born here. They went to school in Thirsk. I have put Darrowby as a composite term in the books. But really – Thirsk is Darrowby." His written tales of a Dales-based vet, in days that now seem long ago, had a wearying round of various publishers and eventually burst on the literary scene with dynamic effect. Who would have thought that a largely fictional account of a vet's life in the 1930s and 1940s would be so sensational?

Alf, vet and scribbler, seemed diffident about his ability and his attainments. He implied that he jotted down his tales in the living room at the end of the day. The Herriot books are too well written to have been impulsive. Each chapter is a meticulously worked short story, with that vital element of conflict to sustain the reader interest. Alf wisely did not cram everything into one book. He developed the theme over several books. As a relative stranger, he could take a dispassionate view of his subject and be aware of the changes in farming practice.

What was the fictitious James Herriot really like? I presumed he had some of the qualities of his creator. Christopher Timothy, who played the part in the long-running BBC television series, told me that when he read the books, he found plenty of descriptions about major characters like Siegfried, Tristan and Helen. Yet hardly anything was written about James himself. "I had to take what little there was and fit a character to it. It pleased me when the real-life James Herriot, in his book about Yorkshire, considered I'd done this well. But it was more luck than judgement..."

The fictional character of Siegfried Farnon, irascible head of the veterinary practice, was based on Alf's real boss whose name was Donald V Sinclair. Before he established himself as a vet in Thirsk, Donald was a Ministry vet in the Settle district of North Ribblesdale. This information came from an elderly lady who remembered him from the 1930s. We had been talking about James Herriot. I had mentioned that Donald's will had just been published, a few months after his death in 1995. The literary Siegfried was on a financial tightrope. So presumably was Donald, but there had been an upswing in his fortunes and he ended his life a rich man, leaving the staggering sum of £1,133,000.

A handsome young vet, Donald had arrived in Settle in 1937 and lodged in a semi-detached house in Duke Street. "The young ladies of the district swooned as they saw him drive round the district in an enormous Lagonda. My mother asked me to be chaperone when Donald took out my elder sister. He was a dashing, sandy-haired figure of great charm. His moustache was like that worn by Errol Flynn, who was a film hero of the time." Keen to improve himself and make more money, Donald departed in 1938 for a practice based on a Georgian house in Kirkgate, Thirsk. In 1939, he advertised for an assistant. The successful applicant was – Alf Wight.

My informant could not recall a choleric side to Donald's manner, as indicated in the Herriot books and as portrayed by Robert Hardy in the BBC series based upon them. Neither could I, judging by the man in his silver-haired old age when we had a brief chat in Leeds on the launch of the book *James Herriot's Yorkshire*.

When the original Herriot books appeared, *The Dalesman* was quick to recognise the authentic touch. We were hardly prepared for universal popularity of these homely tales from the Dales. In a book review of

1971, we commented that Herriot's experiences were lively, unpredictable and often very earthy. They told of the days before modern drugs and chemicals were available, when "every vet had his hypodermic syringe that gave him an air of authority with farmers if not with the animals." Mr Herriot had provided a story that every Yorkshire farmer would enjoy.

I noticed affinities between the Darrowby veterinary set-up, as portrayed by Alf Wight, and the general practitioner's hoose at Tannochbrae, as seen in an adaptation of A J Cronin's *Dr Finlay's Casebook*. Each featured an older man, a young hopeful and a down-to-earth housekeeper. Each book dealt with people who were needed by the entire community.

In 1976, when I visited Pickering, I discovered that filmsters had been to a large house called Houndgate for a cinema version of *All Creatures Great and Small*. It predated the television series. For a time there were dogs rushing through the hall in response to the ringing of the doorbell. Several loads of weeds obscured parts of the three-quarter of an acre garden, which normally is immaculate. Alf Wight had not taken the situation for granted. He had unexpectedly rung the door bell and presented the three sisters who owned Houndgate with an autographed copy of one of his books. Also written in the book was a personal message: "With deepest gratitude for housing my creations."

When the BBC took over Herriot, he was already a world celebrity, thanks largely to an American interest in those cute rural happenings. Each instalment of the series entitled *All Creatures Great and Small* began with a "shot" of moorland, with a winding road; an old-style car, and music to set the feet tapping. The BBC went out of their way to get horned Shorthorn cattle. They managed it by hiring them from an old-style farmer near Barnard Castle. At a time when television productions had become distinctly sleazy, here was a popular programme in which sex was restricted to the animals and violence to harsh words rather than the Hollywood-type punch-up. In this respect, Alf Wight was once again so true to life.

The television films clinched the literary successes and made Alf Wight/James Herriot the best-known vet in the world. The 1930s he described were lean years for farmers as for vets. Indeed, as one Dales farmer told me when we discussed Herriot, at that time he could not have afforded a vet. The few people with "brass" included peke-struck Mrs Pumphrey and her obese, under-exercised, lethargic Tricki-woo, one course of treatment for which – unbeknown to her – was some boisterous exercise with the vet's dogs, plus some rat bites. The peke was returned to its home – and to a welcoming gathering of owner and her friends, plus more rich food.

The lean lands of the Pennines, horned sheep and horned Shorthorn cattle – which Alf Wight referred to as "pretty, gentle animals" – proved gloriously photogenic. It is a pity the BBC picked off-comers to play the main roles for, as Siegfried Farnon said movingly, "the hill farmers are a race apart, proud, independent, spirited." The cast did as well as could be expected. I was motoring from Wensleydale to Swaledale on a high road when I came across a film unit. Also present was Kit Calvert, dalesman extraordinary, holding a pony that his granddaughter was leasing to the BBC for the day. Kit pointed to one of the characters who was dressed up as a labouring type, with sacking round his legs. "He's just asked me if he'd been talking right for t'Dales. He hadn't. But what could I say to him?"

At the outset, there were plenty of good stories to choose from, such as that of the farmer who had a bull suffering from sunstroke. He was relieved that the treatment was not some fancy potion but water, played on the animal from a hosepipe. It was his water. Surely the invoice from the vet would not be heavy. The owner of a pig with a boil on its face must have derived wry amusement from the unsuccessful attempts to capture the squealing animal for treatment. It was left to Tristan, the younger brother of Siegfried, to effect a cure – by losing his temper and chasing the pig in darkness, causing it to brush against a wall and burst the boil.

Do you remember the young vet's encounter with a farmer who had

161

a cupboard laden with home-made wines of every type? Herriot became merry – and was then summoned to a farm owned by devout Methodists, where he attended to a calving under disapproving stares from those who noticed his slurred vowels and behaviour. The courtship of young James Herriot and Helen Alderson had moments of tenderness and highlights of hilarity as fate conspired against the suitor in a variety of small but irritating ways. Having married a farmer's daughter, I was never wholly convinced by the BBC representations of Herriot's young lady.

Dalesfolk were wryly amused by the antics of the filmsters. The only time I watched the filming, an over-assertive production assistant commanded the road traffic to be stopped and everyone to remain quiet for another "take". She did not find it possible to command the RAF to stop flying. A military jet passed with a roar and whoosh of displaced air. I had speculated on the scenes to be filmed. Would James Herriot be portrayed with his arm in the rear end of a cow? Or would we overhear a conversation with a farmer which began with him saying: "Nay, Mr 'Erriot"?

In fact, we were to have tender romance, set in a quiet walled garden. The sound of rooks is among the most English of sounds, but the birds nesting in the big tree must have reached an emotional crisis in their lives. The calls were deafening. The directional microphone was inclined downwards to keep the bird calls to an acceptable level.

By this time, Carol Drinkwater had been succeeded as Mrs 'Erriot by Linda Bellingham. She showed me her real-life, six-week-old baby. Until Herriot entered her life, she had never been to the Dales, though naturally she had read the books about the famous vet. And, of course, she had seen the films. "I had not realised from those films how big and rolling the Dales country really is. I had tended to see it in Postman Pat terms – much smaller than reality." John McGlynn was playing the part of a newcomer to the Darrowby practice, replacing Tristan Farnon, who left – according to the story – to settle in Ireland. John told me his real-life mother nearly fainted with excitement when he got the role.

I chatted with Christopher Timothy who recalled when Robert Hardy as Siegfried, Peter Davidson as Tristan and himself as James Herriot, were to leave the "surgery" in Askrigg. They were instructed to say cheerio to each other and go their separate ways. About 300 people, mainly foreign visitors, were watching the filming. "When we were still inside the front door, I heard "Camera – sound – rolling – and ACTION.

"We opened the front door to absolute silence. All the traffic had been stopped. Then across the front of the house walked a woman carrying two shopping baskets. She was dressed in a costume that was certainly applicable to the period. I heard CUT. I saw the production assistant going across to the lady to ask her if she would mind holding back while the scene was shot. The lady said, very loudly: 'I've got my bloody life to lead, you know.' And, of course, there was no answer to that! It was her village, not ours!"

One of the BBC men I met at Askrigg said: "The Herriot books have affected so many people. The author sat down one day and thought: 'I'll write down all my Dales memories.' The books have benefited publishers, hoteliers, garage proprietor, shop-keepers – US!" James Herriot bore his fame calmly. His outlook towards his animals and other people was unchanged. As a vet, the stock had priority.

He liked nothing better than having time off at West Scrafton, in the dale-country, staying in some small cottage, taking his dogs for walks. In the early days, he broadcast and gave talks to local organisations. Then he had to restrict his public appearances. In addition to his literary activity, he signed myriad books – so many that he was left with defective hands. The Americans came in droves. "Even though I am now retired as a vet, I go down and see them at the surgery," he told me in 1990. "There might be 150 lined up on a Friday. It used to be nearly every day, and then I cut it down to Wednesday and Friday, and now it's just the one day…I never buy and sell my books. We have a wonderful little bookshop in Thirsk. An American runs it. A Texan.

He keeps a good stock."

In our long conversation about his work, I mentioned that his face was "a good colour". He had not been well but seemed "on the mend" and at the mention of "colour", he laughed and recalled his young days as a vet visiting the dalehead farms. "When they said you'd a bad colour, you got worried. I'm not a very ruddy individual really, but they would say: 'Thou's lost a bit o' ground since I saw you last, Mr Wight'. Or: 'I think you've failed a bit, you know'."

After our morning chat, he intended to go walking with one of his oldest friends, who had moved from Glasgow to a home in North Yorkshire. "It's very gradual walking; he and I are of the same age. We just walk and chat and put the world to rights!" Alf Wight has died – but James Herriot lives on, as a literary immortal, locked up in a time-capsule labelled "the Dales in the 1930s and 40s."

If anyone wants a popular account of what dalesfolk were like during those years, which I also remember well, I would simply say: "Read Herriot."